T0333630

HOW
TO
BE
A
DESIGN
STUDENT

(AND HOW TO TEACH THEM)

HOW
TO
BE
A
DESIGN
STUDENT

(AND HOW TO TEACH THEM)

MITCH GOLDSTEIN

PA PRESS

PRINCETON ARCHITECTURAL PRESS · NEW YORK

For all of my students, and all of my teachers, both of whom have taught me far more than I have taught them.

CONTENTS

JARRETT FULLER

When I was a design student, I knew what design was.
I was a precocious teenager, arriving at design school
already having read a handful of design books, and I
could rattle off some famous designers from history. I was
told design was the sensible profession for someone with
an artistic bent, and I agreed. In design school, defining
design was easy: I spent my days picking colors and fonts,
laying out pages and drawing logos. My classmates and I
would laugh at the poor kerning on our dorm's signage—
because that's what designers did. I was going to spend
the rest of my life making magazines or designing book
covers or building websites. I loved it.

But it didn't quite turn out that way. In the fifteen
years since I was a freshman undergraduate design
student, I've designed websites and brands, exhibitions
and books, mobile apps and live events. But I've also

made podcasts, written essays, edited publications, and taught design classes. This strange set of activities I've cobbled together into a career doesn't look like the design I thought I knew when I was eighteen. Yet, for some reason—whether I'm teaching a class or interviewing someone on a podcast, writing a text or editing a book—I still call myself a designer.

As my own work changed, so did the world. The iPhone came out during my first year of college, and Instagram debuted the semester I graduated. The latter would not have been possible without the former, and in the few years immediately after I graduated, new markets and industries were created around these technologies. New possibilities for design opened up. There were opportunities to design in areas that hadn't existed a few years earlier when I was in school, while things I thought I'd be doing had already become obsolete. The tools changed, and the language evolved. Design, it turns out, is so much bigger than I had ever imagined. The truth is, I am still—always, forever—a design student. The title of the book now in your hand—*How to Be a Design Student*—then is misleading. We are all, after all, design students. Fifteen years out, the only thing I can know for sure is that I have no idea what design is.

I met Mitch Goldstein—like I suspect many people did—on Twitter. I immediately felt I had found a kindred spirit. Here was someone else who proudly declared he did not know what design was. Over the years, I've had the joy of talking with Mitch outside of Twitter—on podcasts and phone calls, lengthy emails and Zoom sessions (we will meet in person one day!). We share a bond over the blurriness of design, a greater interest in raising questions than in providing answers, and a belief in the noble act of teaching. Mitch is energized, not intimidated, by the expansiveness of design and its potential. When I've made career changes—from designer to grad student, then grad student to educator—I've asked his perspective and haven't regretted it. Lucky for you, he's packaged the wisdom I've received in those conversations into the book in your hands.

This book doesn't resort to easy definitions and binaries. Instead, it's a book that leans into fuzziness with a generosity, vulnerability, and bigheartedness that feels all too rare. This is not a book that will teach you how to design a logo or build a chair or code an app. You will not learn how to assemble a portfolio that guarantees you a job. What you will learn, however, is how to be and stay curious. You will learn how to embrace confusion and be prepared for whatever is invented right after you graduate. It's a book that helps you make sense of this confusing, energizing, creative, intellectual, frustrating, and incredible time in your life. It gives real, practical advice on topics without oversimplifying or reducing them.

This is the book I wish I'd had when I was a design student, and I can't tell you how happy I am that I have it now, as someone who teaches design students. Because it's a book for teachers, too (we are, after all, students, too!). As design educators, we, too, can—must!—lean into constant change. We can create environments for exploration and experimentation, breakthroughs and failures. We can help create the conditions for students to see design not reductively but expansively. We can cocreate, together with our students, new ways of making and thinking and talking about design.

I often tell my students that I don't know what design is. I also tell them that I firmly believe that each generation's designers get to redefine design for themselves. The design of yesterday isn't the same as the design of today, and that isn't the same as the design of tomorrow. Your time in design school has the potential to be one of the most creative and intellectually stimulating experiences in your life (this is why I teach now). Don't squander it like I did, thinking you have all the answers, thinking you know what design is. Don't spend those four years worrying about grades or jobs or portfolios. Your only job—as a student, as an educator, as a designer, as a human—is to be open to the experience. This, I think, can lead to a long and generative life in design and beyond. This book will give you the tools to begin defining design for yourself. We can learn from each other.

Jarrett Fuller
North Carolina State University College of Design

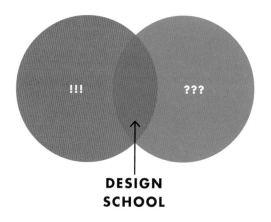

!!!

???

DESIGN
SCHOOL

SHOULD YOU READ THIS BOOK?

College is, to put it lightly, a huge commitment.

A huge commitment of time and money, for sure, but also a huge commitment of your mind: you will work harder and think more deeply during this time than you likely ever have before. Especially if you enroll right out of high school, college may be the first time you have been socially and mentally independent. You will meet many new people, be exposed to new ideas, new cultures, new opinions, new ideologies, new art, new experiences, new books, new music, new environments, new everything.

To put it simply: if you are going to make such an enormous commitment, you need to make it worth it. That is why I wrote this book—to help you get the most out of design school while you are there.

Having taught college students for more than eighteen years, I have spent a long, long time thinking deeply about how I teach, how I learn, how I make art and design, and how teaching, learning, and making are all related to each other in a complex and incredibly interesting way. There is quite a bit of advice out there about what to do while at design school. A quick social media search will bring no shortage of bite-size nuggets of wisdom on how to act as a design student and what to do while you are at school (and more than a few of those nuggets will come from my own social media accounts). What I have not found is a deep, thoughtful, understandable, and accessible book that explores all aspects of how to get the most out of the design school experience, in a way that makes sense for someone either just starting their education, or someone thinking about attending a design school.

This book is based on many successes as a teacher and a student, and many, many, many more failures. It will provide insight for current design students, no matter what stage they are at in their education; offer a guide for those considering going to design school so they can understand what really happens there every day; and help educators teach more interesting and more valuable classes, for both themselves and their students.

Much of this book is written for current and future students, but there are parts that are directed specifically at teachers. I do hope that, whether you are a student or a teacher, you read everything. Teachers and students are deeply intertwined—they are not on two opposing sides.

IF YOU LIKE TO:
MEMORIZE FACTS,
HAVE CLEARLY
DEFINED GOALS,
BE GIVEN
STEP-BY-STEP
DIRECTIONS,
AND BE TOLD
EXACTLY
WHAT TO DO...

FIND ANOTHER
MAJOR.

We are all in it together, working collaboratively to learn how to make and think as creative practitioners. Therefore, it is important to understand what is happening from both perspectives. When a design program is really working well, those two groups of people have an enormous amount in common, with everybody learning and everybody teaching, which is why I have written this as one book, instead of two.

What if you are unsure if you even *want* to be a designer? Maybe you're not sure if you want to go to design school at all. Beyond the practical issues of time and money, is design school a place that would be valuable for you? I will discuss a lot of the ins and outs of what actually happens in your classes: what kind of assignments you can expect, how critiques work, and what you're actually expected to do.

Beyond the day-to-day, I am also going to discuss what lies underneath all the practical, applied, clear stuff design school will teach you — yes, you will learn how to use software, how to translate ideas into paid client projects, how to make things that will get you a job, how to use what you learn as part of your future career. All of this is important, and when you start it seems like this is really what your education will be about. It turns out that this is just the easy stuff that you initially think about, the tip of the iceberg. A lot more happens beyond this, however, and that is what I think separates a *useful* design school experience from an *amazing* design school experience, where you also get to learn all the stuff below the waterline.

Design is a big, ambiguous blob of ideas, methods, tools, concepts, form, content, culture, and the entirety of the human condition. It is also an incredibly wonderful and endlessly interesting thing to learn about and spend your life practicing. This book will help you get there.

Mitch Goldstein
Rochester, New York
July 2022

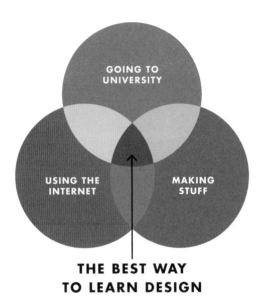

CHAPTER ONE

WHY GO TO DESIGN SCHOOL?

Most people (and especially most parents who are
sending their kid to college) assume that by going to
design school you are purchasing a career. Go to school,
do well, graduate, get a job, live happily ever after.

Getting a job is an excellent reason to get an
education, and working and making money is something
I personally enjoy very much. However, deciding to go
to design school (or really pursuing any higher education
regardless of major) is not about buying a career. The
reality is that despite all the time and money spent, there
is no guarantee that you will get a job when you graduate,
no matter what your school's marketing department says
on the website. What you will get when you decide to
go to design school is an education in creative practice
and active curiosity—which may lead to a job, and very
often does. It is a huge investment without any definitive
outcome, which leads to an incredibly important question

that you have probably already asked yourself, and it's one I hear frequently. It usually goes something like this:

> *Instead of spending all the time and all the money to go to design school and maybe not even getting a job when I leave, why can't I just watch free videos and tutorials online and learn the same stuff?*

It is an excellent question that deserves a real answer. There is a massive amount of information online that will also be covered at school. While much of this information is out there for free, even the paid sites for learning about design cost a tiny fraction of just one semester of college. Learning online is something you can do at home, on your own schedule, any time of day or night. You don't have to move away, or give up your job if you are an older student. Design school (and higher education as a whole) is absurdly expensive—the majority of students will leave with some amount of debt, and some with a huge amount of debt. Many will have to leave their families and move to an unfamiliar place.

Can't you just do it all online instead? The answer is: yes, you can learn to be a designer online. You don't have to go to design school. But, you will not learn the same stuff. YouTube, and paid learning sites such as Skillshare and LinkedIn Learning, have a massive, expansive set of courses—far, far more than could possibly fit into four years of a BFA. You can just keep following the recommendation algorithm forever and learn how to use almost everything. And yes, you can do it in your jammies at 2:00 A.M. with your dog sitting in your lap.

Design school is different; it is an experience that comes with a lot more context and a lot more deeply examined connections within its structure. You have the magical situation of a bunch of people in a room together bouncing ideas off each other, and no, an online chat or the comments section of a YouTube video is *not* the same thing. The importance and value of in-person, face-to-face dialogue and collaboration cannot be understated. I have yet to see anything come close online. Yes, I have been in Slack critique channels, and I have seen Discord servers about design critique, and while these are by no means useless, there is a lot that is missed.

Formal education has a strongly developed curriculum that builds upon itself over many sequential classes. You will also take many classes outside of your specific area of interest, both electives and non-design courses such as liberal arts, writing, sciences, and a full range of others. You will learn way, way more theory and history, especially as very few people trying to learn design online take a history class, or a writing class, or a literature class. This is the education: the stuff beyond the obvious stuff and how these topics all connect together and feed each other in interesting and unpredictable ways.

So, what should you do?

Ideally, you should do both. YouTube and design

school both have lots to offer, and ideally everyone would use both together to get what they need. While the commitment of going to a design program is significant—cost and time and geography are obviously huge issues, especially for those who are not from privileged backgrounds and will have to take out loans to make it happen—it is also valuable. Anyone who tells you that YouTube is a one-to-one substitute for a formal design education and asks, "Why would you possibly pay tens of thousands of dollars when you can do the same exact thing online for free or twenty dollars per month?" is not operating in reality. Both have value. Both offer a way into industry. Both can be good or bad for someone. Setting aside the question of money, either can be the right way or the wrong way to learn.

For me personally, going to design school was a life-changing experience that I desperately needed. I knew I would go into debt even with some family financial support. I was prepared to do so. I would not have gotten remotely close to where I am today without it. I also realize how lucky I was even to be able to attend design school thanks to having emotional, financial, and creative support. I don't take it lightly when I say I am very, very aware of how fortunate I am.

Generally, I believe design school will make students much better creative practitioners and will take them far past where they could go alone. That being said, simply attending design school does not guarantee anything.

There are people who are brilliant and successful who never went to school. There are also people who went to elite design schools who can't design their way out of a paper bag.

And let's bust a myth: I often hear people say that teachers at design schools are antiquated and tired and coasting through teaching while they enjoy tenure and show up on campus to teach one or two days a week. Unfortunately, yes, there are a few teachers like this, but the vast majority of educators—especially in art and design—are active practitioners and insanely curious about their field. A hell of a lot of what educators are paid for is being actively interested in stuff. It is literally in the job description. That old saying "Those who can't, teach" is utter bullshit. The saying should be "Those who can, and can explain why and how they can, teach." I personally look at teaching as a part of my creative practice. It feeds my work and my work feeds my teaching. Much of my motivation is being curious, while much of a YouTuber's motivation is view counts. It is just something to be aware of: understand who is teaching you and why they are doing so.

Conversely there is often a sense among those who teach at design school (especially among older faculty) that YouTube is just a bunch of unqualified kids making worthless videos for the views. This is a gross mis-characterization and incredibly ignorant. There is a massive, valid, highly accessible wealth of knowledge online, and you should not be so quick to dismiss it. Do you need to vet YouTube videos to make sure they are accurate? Sure. But if someone is posting to YouTube they are going to be easily findable online. Look at their portfolio. Check their qualifications. See if they are worth listing to, and—this is really important—you should also do this with your design school teachers.

So to answer the big question: Should you go to design school or just use YouTube?

The answer is simple: Yes.

ART OR DESIGN?

While we are here, let's also discuss some language: What's the difference between "art" and "design," anyway? I have thought about this a lot, spoken with many people, and considered and reconsidered this question for my entire career as a maker and an educator. And, after much debate both with myself and with others, I think I have reached a clear, definitive answer:

It doesn't matter.

Or to put it more accurately: it doesn't matter to me. I don't care what the difference is. This does not mean that art and design are not, in fact, different—it just means that I have never found those differences useful to how I teach and make work. After all, there are many designers who approach their work as art. There are also many artists who approach their work like designers. Labeling a project as one or the other does not give me any useful understanding of what it is and does not help me know what to make or how to make it. I think this unlabeled, fuzzy, ambiguous gray area between art and design is the most interesting place to be. Slapping labels on things and eliminating other ideas or approaches is the most boring place to be, so I won't be doing it in this book, or in my own work, or in my classes.

In this book I will mostly be sticking to the word *design*, but 99 percent of what I speak about here in the context of being a design student can also be applied to being an art student or a craft student or, for that matter, a writing student or a music student—any discipline where we use our creativity and knowledge to make things that don't exist yet.

I bring this up in the first chapter of this book because humans like to put nonverbal things into verbal forms. Words have meaning, and yet art and design are primarily visual or experiential things. While I need words to discuss being a design student in this book, I do not want there to be a semantic debate about what design exactly is or is not.

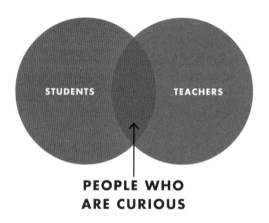

**PEOPLE WHO
ARE CURIOUS**

CHAPTER TWO

LEARNING CURIOSITY

You attend design school to learn how to be a designer, right? That sounds very straightforward, but it raises the question: What will you actually learn?

The answer is rather complicated, but the short version is that you will learn lots and lots and lots of things. No matter which specific discipline of design you major in—graphic, industrial, new media, interactive, spatial (just to name a few)—the basis for all of them is the same. Most undergraduate programs will have you go through some version of a foundation year, which is a catchall term for classes that cover the basics of visual art and design. Usually, you will have classes in drawing, flat or 2D design, sculpture or 3D design, and possibly some time-based design as well (like animation or film). You might also have some general technical classes on software and equipment, in addition to history or other liberal arts classes. But you are not just learning how to draw, or how to make 2D things, or 3D things, or movies. You are not only learning how to use a pencil, or charcoal, or paint, or software, or machinery.

Once you get into your major classes you will learn concepts and methods unique to that major. In graphic design you will learn a lot about typography, branding, publication, interaction, and more. In industrial design you will learn modeling, sketching, fastening, manufacturing, utilizing materials, and much more. This list goes on and on and on. But you are not only learning how to set type or how injection molding works.

I think that every single art and design program at every reputable school is really teaching one thing, in a variety of different ways, over and over: to be actively curious. You are learning how to ask interesting questions and then try to answer them through research, making, ideation, and conversation. Active curiosity is an "applied interest" in something—you are not passively wondering how stuff is done, you are intensely interested and act upon that curiosity to make things. Active curiosity will be the DNA of your creative practice (which we will talk more about later). You will certainly spend a lot of time in design school learning how to do things, the tools to use, the techniques to master, and so on, but underlying all of that is active curiosity. You will learn how to be endlessly curious, but in a way where you can do something with that curiosity.

It is easy—*extremely* easy—for design school to show you how others have done the same thing you are doing, and then teach you how to do it the same way. If this is all you are looking for, you are being trained, not educated. Historical precedent is very important, as everything you will make as a designer has a context, and some of that context is historical, so knowing where things came from, how they came to be, and why they came to be is central to understanding how the world at large affects your work. What is completely unimportant is looking at others' work and thinking, "Well if that's how *Famous Designer* did it, I should do it in a similar way." This is the opposite of learning; this is simply filling out a template someone else created.

Part of learning active curiosity is learning how to make work the way you would do it—not the way your teacher would do it. Not the way *Famous Designer* did it. You are interested in the work, and you are acting on that interest by thinking about what to make, then figuring out how to make it, and then reflecting on what you made and whether it was successful. Active curiosity is about trying to answer interesting questions by making stuff. These questions should never end.

The cool thing about being actively curious is that your teachers are doing the exact same thing. Most students do not realize this, but full-time, tenured or tenure-track teachers have three jobs at a school. Our first job is, of course, teaching: developing projects, going to class every day, critiquing, showing students tools and techniques, explaining concepts, grading, etcetera. The second job is service: all the stuff that students don't see—committee meetings, developing curricula, doing portfolio reviews, putting together exhibitions for students, serving on things like academic senate, etcetera. We serve the program we are teaching in as well as the university and really the entire field of design beyond school. The third job (the most relevant to what I am talking about in this chapter) is research (sometimes called scholarship): the stuff that requires active curiosity. Research can look like a million different things: sometimes it is creating work as a designer, sometimes it is teaching workshops and lecturing about things at conferences and other institutions, other times it's working on initiatives outside of the classroom. Often research is writing books or articles about the discipline we are in. Regardless of exactly what it looks like, research is being actively curious in what we do as educators and designers, and that is literally a part of our job; we are being paid to be curious.

So, when I say that part of your role as a student is to be actively curious, I mean it. This is coming from my own experience as both a former and current student and an educator. As I write this book, I am in the middle of pursuing another master's degree in furniture design at

RIT. Curiosity is part of what makes a good student a good student, and a good teacher a good teacher.

FOR TEACHERS, I think it is very important to let students into your own creative practice so they can see and understand your curiosity. As an example, I really enjoy posting my work on social media to allow students to know what I'm working on and to let them see the inside of my brain (to some extent). There are lots of good reasons I do this, not the least of which is it helps me more clearly understand what I'm doing in my own work by seeing it through their eyes. Generally one of the first things I do at the beginning of the semester is show students my social media accounts, and I encourage them to take a look at my work, take a look at my writing, take a look at what I'm thinking about and talking about, take a look at what I have to say, and then decide for themselves if I'm worth listening to or not. This shows that I am not distanced from the experience they are all having. Instead, it helps them clearly understand that I am exactly where they are and I know exactly what it is like, because I am doing the same things they are.

Social media, streaming platforms, and the Internet in general are all amazing ways to talk about your interests that can reach a massive audience far, far beyond just the students in your classroom. I use social media constantly, and this is why I was asked to write this book — I've been spending years talking about teaching art and design in an open, accessible, and public way on the Internet. Explaining what I'm thinking about in small, social media–friendly bite-size nuggets has turned out to be an excellent way for me to understand what I'm doing both inside and outside of the classroom. If I want to teach a specific idea, explore something interesting I just discovered, or show something useful I want students to know about, I don't have to write it into my curriculum and then wait three semesters to get a class I can teach it in. I can just write a tweet or upload a YouTube video and immediately get it in front of people.

Behind the scenes (and what people don't usually realize) is that everything that I post on the Internet is first directed at me — me as a teacher, me as a student, me as a practitioner, and me as someone trying to understand what I'm doing in the world. Students frequently tell me how much they appreciate something I've said online, because it offers additional context to what I'm saying in my classes and helps them understand that I am not just casually teaching to cash a paycheck and get summers off. I am doing this because I can't not do this. It is what I'm here to do, and posting interesting things at ten o'clock on a Tuesday night in July proves my commitment. Social media offers an open, honest, unrestrained, and unfiltered opportunity to speak about what I am doing and what I am trying to do — and this is not only very good for me but also very good for my students. They understand that I am right where they are, trying to figure it out every day. This makes me a lot less authoritarian and a lot more approachable in the classroom, and it also makes my students realize that I truly empathize with their struggles, because I am having the same struggles.

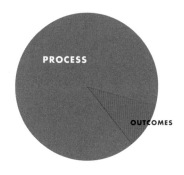

PROCESS

OUTCOMES

WHAT YOU FOCUS ON
AT DESIGN SCHOOL

CHAPTER THREE

PROCESS AND PRACTICE

Let's get off campus for a second. What does a professional designer actually do, anyway? You are coming to design school to learn how to be a creative professional in any number of different fields, so you have to be wondering: What is the job really like? What are the expectations and goals of working as a designer? This can look very different depending on lots of factors: the field, the location, the market, and the kind of place you work, whether it's in-house or for a design studio. But generally speaking, no matter the specifics, all design jobs share a few similarities and common goals.

First and foremost: professional practice is a business, and a primary goal of a business is to be profitable and make money. A lot of time is spent on money — making budgets and bidding on projects. Invoicing, collecting, and accounting for money. Paying expenses and employee salaries. Buying equipment, supplies, software, office furniture, and everything it takes to run a business. Making money, spending money, and accounting for the money made and money spent takes time and…money. This attention to money applies just as much for a single freelancer as it does for a huge agency—the scale of the numbers may differ, but the general idea is the same.

Second, the goal of professional practice is not primarily learning, it is executing what you have already learned. Clients and studios hire you because they assume you already know what you need to know in order to complete the projects they are hiring you for. As a human who is curious, yes, of course you will always be learning new things—but that is not the point of them hiring you. They hire you to complete a job, which they expect you to be able to do on time and within the parameters the client has set, be it within a tight budget, too little time, or more often both.

Last, professional practice is generally focused on the needs of the client and their audience by way of the deliverable thing you give them at the end of the project. They are hiring you to make a thing that satisfies the needs of their business and the people who spend money at their business. Design is a service industry, and you are paid for your services—that is, making things your clients need. Part of that is knowing how to communicate with a client, how to talk about your ideas, how to listen to their ideas and needs, and how to translate that into things.

This is often forgotten by students and their teachers: design school is not commercial practice. The goals of school are almost the exact opposite of the goals of a job. The goal of school is to learn, not to be profitable. You do not have clients, you have teachers and classmates. The final thing you make is so often less important than how you got there. Commercial practice is mostly concerned about the destination, whereas school is mostly concerned about the journey. You will absolutely make "final" things in your classes. You will do research to understand the needs of the audience you have been given in your assignments. You will do a lot of things that parallel what you will do in professional practice. You will not ignore the world beyond school, but you will shift focus to the process of making. Does this mean the final stuff you make does not matter, as long as you had an interesting process? Sometimes, yes. In my own classes, very often yes.

The reason why there is such a strong focus on process during school is that it takes a lot of practice to understand how certain decisions at the start of a project affect the outcome. Making decisions—hundreds or thousands of decisions in one project—is part of the process of making work, and it takes time to learn how to make useful decisions. You do not get a project, figure out exactly what the final outcome should be in a few minutes, and then just spend your time making that exact outcome. Design does not work like that. There is a long, deep, involved process that goes into it, and having a really good process will help you make really good work. Creating a design process is something you have to learn how to do, and that is why the focus at school is so much on process instead of just outcome—this is where you learn how to do it, through a lot of testing, trial and error, experimentation, and just doing stuff and seeing what happens. Sometimes what happens is good, sometimes it is not.

At school there is a huge, important benefit to making "bad" stuff: making bad stuff helps you understand how to make the good stuff. But in commercial practice you are always expected to make the good stuff. No client is going to hire you with the understanding that you will make lots of bad stuff as part of the process—they assume you already did that while you were at school. This is why it is all in the process: as a student you will spend a lot of time thinking about and talking about the choices you make, why you made them, and what the results of those choices were. This is how you start to diverge from your classmates—in making the choices that you make, you will make the kind of work you want, which can be very, very different from the choices and the work of the person next to you. Understanding why your choices shape your work in a certain way is critically important, and you will spend your entire career figuring this out.

IT'S CALLED
"CREATIVE
PRACTICE"
BECAUSE
YOU NEVER
STOP LEARNING
HOW TO
DO IT.

A term you may hear a lot both at school and in commercial work is *creative practice*. This catchall term means all the stuff you do as a designer and artist—the work you make, the projects you complete, the topics you research, the meetings with clients or commissions—all of this is your creative practice. However, there is a lot more nuance to it than just "this is all this stuff I do." Creative practice is really a direct extension and continuation of school and curiosity, but out of school, you no longer have assignments, dorms, finals week, grades, and all of the many distractions of being at college. Instead, you have the ability to focus on exactly what you are deeply and passionately curious about. Your job can be (and ideally should be) a part of your creative practice, but it does not have to be; it can be the thing you do for money outside of your practice.

Your creative practice could focus on what you do outside of work, and it may not even focus exactly on the discipline you studied at school. Your BFA in graphic design might be what helps you get a job as a graphic designer and pay your bills, but your creative practice might be painting, writing, music, sculpture, performance, ceramics, or a million other things that are tangentially related to, but not the same as, what your degree is in. In addition to teaching, I also create design, make fine art, do a lot of writing, speak at events and schools, run workshops, and so on and so forth. I consider all of this my creative practice, and it all mixes together in one big giant ball of interesting things I enjoy.

What you're learning in school is a lot more than the pragmatics of being a designer—the tools, techniques, rules, and how to be a "professional." Those things are extremely valuable, and you really do have to know them—if you cannot execute your ideas, they are not of much value to anyone, including you. You have to learn the applied parts of your discipline: Is knowing which typeface to use for a specific kind of mood or tone important? Absolutely. Is knowing the properties of a material you are thinking about using for a consumer product important? Of course. Is learning how to test designs with focus groups important for user experience projects? Unquestionably. The application is one leg of your creative practice, the one most people see.

However, creative practice is about much more than just the tangible, practical, applied, deliverable work you externalize (and hopefully get paid for). Once again, let's use the iceberg metaphor: what everyone sees sticking out of the water is just a small part of what goes into making work, and creative practice is exploring the whole iceberg, including everything below the waterline that nobody but you gets to see. Ultimately what you do for the rest of your life as a creative practitioner is both practical and conceptual, both the thinking and the application.

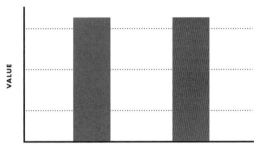

CHAPTER FOUR

DISCOMFORT

At college, most people are thrown into a group of people they have never met before but will spend the next few years with, learning and growing together. You will be grouped with people from different backgrounds, different places, different educations, and different skills. You will soon start to realize that everyone learns differently. The good news is that there is no "right" way to be a student. The bad news is also that there is no "right" way to be a student. Even though you are reading a book right now that is literally about *how to be a design student*, I have no expectation that everything I say will apply to every student universally; everyone processes the experience differently. This is what makes design school so incredibly interesting from the perspective of a teacher: there is no "right" way to be a design teacher, either. I always experiment with my classes and try different things in the hopes of everyone getting something from the class. Every student should try to be aware of what kind of student they actually are, in terms of their personality, their process, and their goals and wishes. Knowing how you learn best and what does and does not work for you will help you navigate your education and help you let your teachers know what you need to get the most out of your time.

Some students are outgoing and convivial. You know this kind of student: they always have a comment during critique (some of which are useful and insightful and some of which are not). This is the student who loves group projects, who ends up running a club or organization, who you can always hear talking to other students in studio after class. Other students are more reserved. They may be much quieter during crits and avoid leadership roles. They might like independent work more than group projects. In the same way that there are different kinds of students, there are also different kinds of teachers. The exact same set of characteristics applies—there are teachers who are loud and outgoing and those who are quieter and more reserved. Some teachers thrive on leading big group critiques, and others much prefer to meet with students one-on-one. Some are very experimental and ambiguous; others are more goal- and rule-oriented.

Regardless of which kind of student you are or which kind of teacher you have, there are things to be aware of as you go through school. Since neither of these is the "best" kind of student or teacher, neither approach is bad or good. You do not have to be outgoing to make great work. You do not have to prefer being alone to make great work. Since neither end of the spectrum is a goal to achieve, you can lean into who you are. Consider the kinds of projects and classes and teachers you are picking and cater them toward your personality. We all learn differently, so gearing your education to serve how you learn can be a good strategy. Differences are what make design school, and design in general, extremely interesting. If everybody had the exact same personality, learned the same exact way, and did the exact same kinds of things, school would get extremely boring, extremely quickly. Differences are good. Knowing what you want out of a class or a teacher—and being able to let your teacher know that—can help you feel comfortable in the class and maybe get a lot more out of the experience.

This does, however, present a serious problem: discomfort is also valuable. School is an excellent place to be awkward and uncomfortable in your work. To some extent, comfort can lead to stagnation and predictability—yes, it may be more aligned to what you think you want and need, but that can do more harm than good. How can you grow if you do not try new, uncomfortable things? Leaning into the discomfort will likely help you grow far beyond what you could do if you stuck with the familiar and safe. No matter where you end up working after graduation, whether for yourself as an independent designer, in-house at a non-design company, or for a large, cool, hip agency, you will rarely be able to tailor your day-to-day existence. Even if you decide to work for yourself, you will still have client relationships to navigate, and they will not all go the way you want them to. So, there is something extremely valuable to being very uncomfortable with how you learn. It will help you be more flexible, agile, and empathetic to other designers and clients.

With all of this in mind—and this goes for students and teachers—you should embrace both the comfort and the discomfort. It is not healthy to be constantly and endlessly uncomfortable and on edge the entire time you are at school—that can become damaging emotionally and physically. It is also equally unhealthy to always feel safe and perfectly in your comfort zone—so you become stagnant and float through your classes. You should seek out places to be both comfortable and uncomfortable. This extends to your life both while at school and after. You can strive to have a very calm home life if that gives you a stable foundation to be awkward and uncomfortable in your work. The point here is that you need the contrast of both comfort and discomfort for each of them to be more valuable. You want to avoid an easy, predictable, and neutral design school experience.

FOR TEACHERS, despite how counterintuitive this sounds, you should *not* just teach in your comfort zone and about topics that you feel incredibly comfortable with. A lot of teaching is about helping students ask interesting questions and then helping them find the answers. When you know a topic inside and out, when you have taught the same class or the same projects over and over and over, you stop seeing the interesting questions. It becomes impossible to see what you are teaching with fresh eyes. Teachers need to be students at least as much as their students need to be students.

Even if you teach a class that you have taught many times before, you should not just repeat the same projects over and over every semester. Experiment, try new prompts, and make sure to accept that just as students can screw up projects, so can teachers. That doesn't mean your new project was not valuable; this does not mean you and your students won't learn an awful lot from a project that crashes and burns. Art and design education is about as far as you can get from an exact science, and as an educator you should use that to your advantage. One of the worst things you can do as an educator is to stagnate—while every semester a new crop of students experiences your class for the first time, it is far too easy to just change the dates on your syllabi and teach what you have taught before. Changing things up will keep your perspective fresh and the class exciting for you and your students, and it will help you find new ways to talk about design.

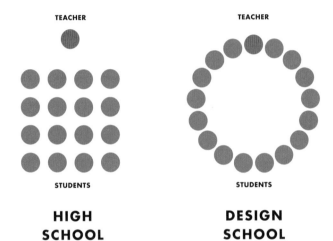

TEACHER

STUDENTS

**HIGH
SCHOOL**

TEACHER

STUDENTS

**DESIGN
SCHOOL**

CHAPTER FIVE

TEAMMATES

There is a style of teaching known in education circles as "the sage on a stage." This is shorthand for the attitude that the teacher knows all the stuff and that the students need to absorb as much of this knowledge as possible. Therefore, the teacher stands up in front of the class in a lecture hall and talks while the students all try to write down everything they say and remember it all. While a fair bit of this does still exist in higher education, it is clearly an antiquated idea: teacher knows everything and student knows nothing.

The sage on a stage scenario happens a lot less in art and design schools, and that is because any good art and design educator does not just stand in front of the room talking. Good educators are in the trenches with their students. They are also asking questions, finding new ways to think about their field, seeing which choices work and which don't, and using inquiry to discover new stuff.

They are in partnership with their students, teammates working toward the same goal—making great work. Unlike the sage on a stage, they make no pretense of knowing all the answers or holding all the knowledge. A good design teacher discovers answers right alongside their students.

This is usually a really big surprise for college freshmen coming from a standard K through 12 education, who are generally very used to tests and exams and papers and twelve-plus years of things that are right and things that are wrong. They understand that the teacher is the ultimate authority and decider of good or bad in the classroom. They have been used to trying to impress the teacher with the right answer at the right time. The idea that the teacher might also not know the answer seems absurd. If they don't know the answer, what business do they have teaching?

Now we circle back to the idea of curiosity and process: so very often art and design are not about finding the right answer—they are about asking an interesting question and figuring out ways to answer it. Design is a lot less about facts than most disciplines. There are far more fuzzy gray areas, and that's what makes it such an incredibly interesting field to be in. This is also what can make it a frustrating field to learn (and, if we are being honest, to teach). Students want to be guided, told what to do, and given clear directives on what way is the right way and what way is the wrong way.

This does not mean that good teachers have no idea what they are doing. Really good design educators are not ignorant—quite the opposite. All good teachers have a deep and applied understanding of their discipline. Graphic design teachers fully understand typography and image. Interior design teachers have knowledge and experience in spatial relationships, materials, textures, and so on. They know the field they are teaching very well, and they can clearly and usefully help their students learn and understand the established principles of that field. They have a deep well of knowledge of the "rules" of their discipline (and when to break them).

Really good design teachers also know when it is time not to know. When not to give the easy answer or the clear direction. They understand that in the quest to learn, sometimes simply giving answers is the least valuable lesson. I often do this in my classes: after giving an assignment, a student (usually many students) will start a question with something like "Is it okay if I ____?" I look them in the eye and say, "That's a great question!" and then turn to the next student and ask, "Any other questions?" This is not a funny joke written just for this book—I really do this all the time in my classes. As you can imagine, this does not go over well. The students get annoyed that I will not just tell them what to do. I have to admit that while I delight in messing with their heads a bit, it really is a valuable lesson in process; it is me saying, "I don't know whether that's okay. Try it and let's find out!"

This is the key thing to understand about the relationship between student and teacher at design school: the teacher almost never knows the correct answer because there is so rarely a correct answer to know. You are all in it together.

FOR TEACHERS, this may just sound like silly semantics, but it is really important: insist that your students call you by your first name. I understand and appreciate the cultural respect that being called "Professor Goldstein" signifies. I know I have worked very hard to earn that title, and it doesn't irritate me that students want to call me "Professor," but I think it represents a breakdown of the partnership teachers should have with their students. Yes, I am their professor, but first and foremost I am just Mitch. For some students who just cannot bring themselves to call me only by my first name, I am "Professor Mitch," which is close enough. It is extremely important for students to understand that I am just a person who likes to make stuff, and likes to help others learn how to make stuff as well. I am in it with the students—I am not above them, I am not removed from their struggle, I am very much right next to them in almost identical circumstances, despite being the teacher of the class. The sooner that you can break that professor/student barrier, the sooner you can start acting as your students' teammate.

There certainly is a place for that authority: grading, writing recommendations, developing curricula. It is not useless or invalid, and sometimes you will need to be Professor You. What you do not want to do is establish a hard boundary between you and your students during the day-to-day of the class—this makes it harder to empathize with your students and harder to teach them.

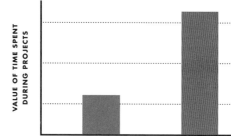

PULLING

It is Day One, and you, the student, sit in the classroom or studio, ready to get started. You are excited. You are nervous. You can't believe you are actually in college. So, what happens now?

Here is what a lot of people think happens: you are about to be told everything you will ever need to know about how to be a successful designer. You will be given projects and assignments that will test you on exactly what you have to understand to go get paid as a designer. Your teachers will tell you what to do and the exact right way to do it. You will pay close attention, write it all down, memorize it, and then recite it back to your teacher, and by doing exactly what they say, you will hopefully get an A for your efforts. All you need to do is whatever your teachers tell you, and you will have a perfect GPA and get an amazing job as a designer when you graduate in exactly four years.

What students want—especially first year students—is to be told the "right" way to do everything. This is a method of teaching that I call *pushing*: information being delivered to students by their teachers in a way that dictates its legitimacy and correctness. Students want to be told "This is exactly the best way to do this" by their teacher, and then they can just duplicate that and get an A. There will and should always be a part of design school that is pushing—as someone who wants to be an applied practitioner you have to learn good techniques, technical skills, and best practices in your discipline to be able to work professionally. You need to learn good craft and how to apply your ideas to the world outside of your mind. There is a practical, pragmatic, and applied value in aspects of your design education being pushed on you.

Pushing should not be the majority of your design school experience. Any time spent in any good design program is almost the exact opposite of this. Simply being pushed information is not what you are in school for, and what makes all of this a really big change—and often an incredibly difficult one—is that a lot of education before college is exactly what I mentioned above, especially in non-art classes. I teach a lot of freshmen, and when they realize they are not going to be told what to do, it is a huge moment. I can see fear in their faces when I don't explain exactly how to get an A.

Design school must include a lot of pulling—students should be asking questions and then seeking their own answers for what is "right" and "wrong." You should try things that you are not sure will work, are not sure are "correct," and are not sure the teacher will like. You should do things because you are actively curious, not just because that is what you've been told to do. Good design students learn to take and not just wait to receive. This is what separates the people who are simply attending college from the people really invested in what they are doing. Students who get the most out of their design school experience are constantly pulling from their teachers and their classmates, because they are constantly thirsty for knowledge.

You are at design school to become educated, not trained, and there is a big difference between the two. Training teaches you how to do a specific set of pre-defined or predictable things very well. It is about hard edges, and proficiency in something we can point at and say, "You need to know how to do that." Education teaches you how to do things that don't exist yet and is about having a much deeper understanding of ideas and context, as well as processes and methods. Design school is all about being educated as a designer, so you can work on projects that are not simply cut and paste, with clear, easy-to-understand goals and deliverables. Education will allow you to think laterally and abstractly about what you are doing and teach you how to tackle those fuzzy gray areas that cross over each other in unexpected ways. Training will help you get your very first entry-level job, but education will last a lifetime. As a person who is getting educated, you will have to learn to work within uncertainty, ambiguity, and abstraction, because that is what pulling is all about—you don't know what to do, so you try something and see what happens.

FOR TEACHERS, think about how you are presenting assignments to your students. Are your project sheets many pages long, with numbered step-by-step directions, extremely specific descriptions of what the desired outcomes are, and hard parameters students must adhere to? This is an assignment that is centered in pushing rather than pulling; you are basically saying, "This is how you do this assignment, this is how you get to the finish line, and this is what the finish line more or less needs to look like." There are certainly important and valuable things to be learned by detailed, specific projects like these, as designers must learn how to work within a tight set of restrictions. As I mentioned above, these projects are fine as long as they are not in the majority, especially as students develop and move through the design program.

Try following up a prescriptive project with one that is extremely open, allowing students to see how they can move from working within restrictive parameters to working with more ambiguous ones. My favorite kinds of projects in this vein are simply one-sentence prompts with a deadline, and that's it. Obviously, this does not work for all assignments in all classes or for all levels of students, but I think the attitude of allowing for a lot of interpretive, wiggly gray areas in your projects is extremely important. It makes sense within one class to give a pushing assignment followed by a pulling assignment; this keeps the class interesting and dynamic and provides a lot of perspectives on creating work within the confines of a single subject.

I have also run pushing and pulling projects at the same time. Doing this will depend a bit on how your institution schedules classes. Many of the schools where I have taught schedule twice-weekly studio classes rather than a single long weekly meeting (if you meet once a week you can use this technique by splitting the day in half). For example, I teach typography. My Tuesday class meeting will focus on a pushing project, typically teaching technical aspects of type or established typographic guidelines, projects such as making a "perfect" type-specimen poster. My Thursday class meeting will explore a much more opened-ended, abstract, expressive pulling project, like creating typographic album covers or concrete poetry. Teaching pushing and pulling simultaneously makes students clearly understand that design is not a "one or the other" kind of discipline— it is a "both at the same time" kind of discipline. There is value in pulling and pushing and every designer (and teacher) needs to do both.

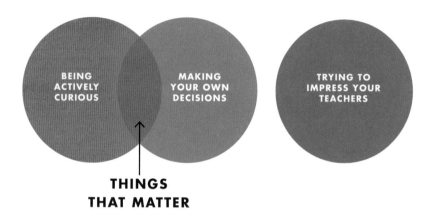

BEING ACTIVELY CURIOUS

MAKING YOUR OWN DECISIONS

TRYING TO IMPRESS YOUR TEACHERS

THINGS THAT MATTER

CHAPTER SEVEN

AGENCY AND YOU-NESS

One of the biggest and most important things you need
to learn as a design student is to have *agency*. In this case,
"agency" is not the cool studio in Brooklyn you go work
at after you graduate. Agency is about being independent,
about making your own decisions, and about directing
your own education. To have agency means to have an
implicit investment in what you are doing. It is about
ownership and possession—you must own what you
make, how you make it, and why you make it, whether
it is good or bad. *Agency* is having your voice in the work
you make and having authorship in what you are creating.
It means learning how to take action and make decisions
rather than waiting for instruction. It is about having
a real intent with your work rather than just doing what's
popular right now.

One of the great things about design as a discipline
right now in the twenty-first century is that it has become

extremely accessible. The very same tools and software people at the top of the profession use are readily available to a high school student. You are one social media follow away from talking to a superstar designer that you admire. You can work as a designer from anywhere, for anyone, at any time. The world has become very, very small in a lot of ways, and design has tied this together. This is fantastic: there is far less gatekeeping in the field. You don't have to attend the exact right school, know the exact right people, and be super lucky to be able to work as a designer. It is a wide-open field. The act of designing is something every human being does every day one way or another; it is quite simply just a part of living in the world right now.

A flyer made by a fourteen-year-old with a word processing program to advertise their grandmother's yard sale and a multimillion-dollar branding and identity campaign from a huge studio in New York City are both considered "graphic design." They both fall under the same discipline—obviously the scale is different, but putting aside scale and money, the real difference is agency. The fourteen-year-old does not have the same level of agency that the creative director at a studio has in making graphic design. The fourteen-year-old is not as invested in the practice of design, is not taking the deeper dive, and is not asking really difficult and challenging questions with the work.

Learning to have agency as you go through design school is what will later separate the true practitioners from the people who are just punching a clock, or doing design as a hobby, or who happen to own some software and have watched a couple of tutorials. Cultivating agency will help you develop into someone who can work far beyond the simple mechanics and technical production of design and become a more inquisitive, curious, and active practitioner who does interesting things. It will also help you develop a sense of self and authorship in the work you make; that is, it will help you develop your voice as a designer and your opinion about design. Lastly, it will help you approach design as a creative practice rather than just a jobby job pushing pixels around all day. Agency encompasses every part of how you approach your education and will make you become an active, engaged, invested participant in your education, not just someone who sits there and hopes they did the right thing to get an A.

Parallel to developing agency is developing you-ness while you are at school. One thing that I never want to teach a student is how to be more like me. I already have a very healthy ego. What I want to teach students is how to be themselves. I want them to be able to do work the way they would work, not the way I would work. I want them to learn how to make decisions the way they would make decisions, not the way they think I want them to make decisions. I don't want my students to spend any time at all emulating me or anybody else—I want them to learn how to be who they are and figure out what their own work looks like.

There's this idea—especially in design—that you need to be separated from the work you create, that the work is just something you make but it is not really a reflection of you. There's a lot of talk about "only serving the needs of the client" and that your opinion, your personality, and your beliefs have no business whatsoever in client projects—that you must have distance from your work and remember that the work is in no way personal. It is just business.

This is absolutely absurd.

Design is not neutral, and the kind of projects you take on, the kind of people you work with, the kind of things you create, the way you make things—everything you do when it comes to design—is a manifestation of your opinion about design and creative practice. Everything you make has you-ness—and part of what you will do at design school is develop this you-ness as you develop skills as a designer. You are absolutely in your work. It does not matter if you are making work for a client, for an agency, for your grandparents, or for yourself—your work is always a reflection of you and what you care about. Just because someone is paying you to create work for their business does not mean you disappear. It is the exact opposite—they are hiring you for a reason, and you bring something unique to the table that another designer does not.

I fully understand the logic of trying to completely separate from your work. To some extent it makes sense: picking a bad typeface does not mean you are a horrible person. Having a rough time designing a website layout does not mean you are a worthless human being. This is the same kind of separation that needs to happen during a design critique (see Chapter 10: Critique). Criticisms are not judgments about your humanity, they are only judgments about the design work you made. That being said, the idea that a designer can have complete and perfect objectivity and no personal investment when it comes to creating work with a client or employer is ridiculous. The process of creating design is too deeply intertwined with the specific human mind that is creating it—and all of its faults and opinions—to possibly think they can be fully removed from each other.

It is clear that clients or agencies hire designers for specific reasons. Maybe those reasons are purely pragmatic—you know how to do a certain thing the client needs, have skills with a certain software, or have experience within a certain kind of industry. Maybe the reasons are interpersonal: they like you as a person, you work well with other people, you're great at collaborating and working on teams. Ultimately you are being hired for your you-ness. If you-ness did not matter, then any qualified designer could create any kind of design for any client in any style anywhere in the world. And that is just not true.

FOR TEACHERS, helping students develop their you-ness is surprisingly difficult. After all, you already know how you make work. You know what sorts of decisions work for you, and as a good teacher who wants to help students become better, you are naturally inclined to tell your students how you would do stuff. This is not inherently problematic. However, what so often happens, especially with teachers who have large personalities (like yours truly), is that students get into the habit of always waiting for you to explain how you did it. When this happens, they are not learning how to be themselves—they are learning how to be you.

I try to help students develop their sense of self by directing as little as possible, and I avoid making definitive right/wrong or yes/no statements as much as possible. I have some knowledge that students can use, and I do want them to know the things that I know, but not in a "this is how it is done" kind of way. One of my favorite things that happens during a project is not when a student does something exactly the way I told them to—it is when they do something exactly the opposite of the way I told them to and it still turns out successful and interesting. That student has developed a sense of you-ness in that moment, and that is far, far more valuable than being able to perfectly duplicate what I do in my own work.

One last thing: I absolutely refuse to refer to college students as kids. They are not kids. All they are is younger than the instructor (and sometimes they are older). Referring to them as kids, treating them like kids, talking about them like they are kids makes them feel like kids, strips them of their agency and responsibility to make decisions for themselves, and inherently says that they should wait for the grown-ups (in this case, their teachers) to tell them what to do. I not only think this is wrong, I think it is repulsive, offensive, and hinders the learning process. My students get treated like adults. They are responsible for their own decisions, and they learn how to be themselves very, very quickly in my classes. If eighteen is old enough to vote in an election and die in a war, it is old enough to not be called a kid by a design teacher.

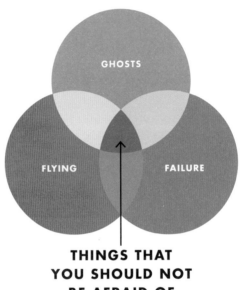

**THINGS THAT
YOU SHOULD NOT
BE AFRAID OF**

CHAPTER EIGHT

FAILURE

Pulling, agency, you-ness…these all sound good and make sense, but are very, very difficult to actually learn, especially for new design students. They have spent the majority of their early education being pushed, and to suddenly be asked to take full ownership of their work and to make decisions without asking the teachers if it is okay first is a huge jolt. So, as a student, you are now asking yourself: How exactly do I actually do this?

The answer is quite simple: don't be afraid of failure.

We live in a goal-oriented culture, where you are always expected to be the best, to be at the top, and to win. Failure, as they say, is not an option. This expectation comes from a lot of places: first from your parents, who were also taught that failure is not an option. It comes from our culture of sports and competition and politics, all of which focus on winning. It also comes from our contemporary consumer culture—

sayings like "The person who dies with the most toys wins" and "Winning isn't everything, it is the only thing" are perfect examples. So of course, you come to school thinking that you can't fail at anything, because you have been taught that for your entire life. In college it seems like failure is the worst possible thing that could ever happen to you. There is no worse event in the entirety of your education than failing at something.

The good news is that school is the best possible place to make the worst work you have ever made. You are inside a place of making and critique, where you have teachers and classmates who are all there for the same reason: to learn. (Yes, good teachers are there to learn as much as to teach.) In design school, failure can be incredibly valuable and, I would argue, necessary. That being said, you should not intentionally try to fail. The goal here is not failure, it is learning—and from failure, you can learn a lot.

That is why, when it comes to failing, it is really important to fail usefully. For failing to be worth it, you have to glean value from the failure, and that value is not a good grade or a cool portfolio piece but instead a lesson learned. Failure is an excellent way to get your work to a place you could never plan on, one you would never get to if you ended up doing your project "correctly." When used well, failure not only means that you have figured out a way to not do a project, it means you have also used it as a spark for new ideas, which is

AN EXCELLENT
WAY TO MAKE
GREAT WORK
IS TO NOT
BE AFRAID
OF MAKING
BAD WORK.

really one of the best things about failing: the ideas that come out of it. Ultimately you have to allow for failure as part of your process because to allow for failure is to allow for new ideas, for things you didn't think of to bubble up.

I think it is impossible to make really great work without first making absolutely awful work. Truly great work comes when you transcend the expected, when you go off of a predictable path into really unexpected territory. Predictable work can be very competent, it can be "good" work, but I don't think it can be truly great. To get your work past good and into great, you have to try new stuff, you have to do things that have not previously been done over and over and over again by all the designers before you. Therefore, you have to try new things, and to try new things, to push boundaries, to experiment, to try stuff that just might not work, means some of it—maybe a lot of it—is going to suck. Failing at this kind of stuff is a cost of doing business. It is a part of the creative process, and that is not necessarily a bad thing if you can get value from it.

The big problem with failing is that it almost always feels awful. When you have worked hard on something and it fails, you are miserable; you feel irritated at spending all this time on something that didn't work. You feel like you screwed up something you should know how to do and like you're never going to make anything good ever again for the rest of your life. Hopefully this feeling lasts just a few minutes, but sometimes it takes many days, months, or even years. This is why you have to practice at failing. You have to understand that just because you screwed something up does not mean you are horrible at what you're doing and you should quit.

The great news about being an artist or designer is that generally we don't die when we make crappy work. The stakes are just not that high, especially in school, where I would argue the stakes of any one project are extremely low. If you screw up one project in one class in one semester in one year of class out of your four years of undergraduate school…it essentially means nothing. Look at it this way: at an average undergraduate design program, you will take three studio classes a semester, each with three to five projects per semester. In four years, that's around one hundred projects—so failing one here and there is not going to affect that much. Really, you will rarely fail at the very end just in time for the final grade. Instead, you will probably fail a lot in the beginning, get over the hump of misery, figure out something interesting, and then wind up with something good by the end of the project.

FOR TEACHERS, you must create an environment that allows students to fail, and I would even say an environment that encourages them to fail, but in a way that teaches them something. One of my favorite ways to do this is by assigning projects where they have to make a lot of stuff in a relatively short amount of time. My all-time favorite project—and a project that has gotten something of a reputation around RIT, where I teach—is the "Obstructions" project. Students have to pick a bunch of ridiculous and absurd limitations out of a bag and then create a thing a day for as many as five or six weeks. Another favorite project I like to give freshmen (that has also gained a reputation among art and design students) is the "Surface" project: students have to make "recordings" of the environment around them by physically rubbing, pressing, manipulating, or otherwise altering one hundred letter-size pieces of copy paper with their environment each week for two weeks.

Both of these projects result in a lot, and I do mean a lot, of failure: pieces that basically just look like garbage. But within all of the garbage students make, some absolutely incredible, amazing things happen— students learn new ideas, processes, and materials, and every student makes at least a few incredibly interesting things. These projects result in a lot of useful failure and learning, making freshman year extremely valuable. Many students come back to me when they graduate and tell me how much they thought these projects were completely idiotic when they did them as freshmen but that they later realized how valuable they were as they got deeper into their majors.

Another thing you can do as a teacher to encourage useful failure is to grade on risk: the more risks they take with their project, the better their grade. I do this in conjunction with other project goals (see the next chapter for more on grading), but I make sure students understand that I want them to take risks with their project, I want them to try stuff that might crash and burn. Projects can be risky in many different ways. Sometimes it could be the content or subject matter they choose to work with. They could decide to try risky tools, techniques, or processes. They could work with risky ideas or concepts. No matter what they do, I am encouraging them to just go for it, see what happens, and expect that some of what they create is going to be bad, but they can learn from it. As soon as they realize that I am serious—that they will not be punished for screwing up—stuff starts getting really, really interesting.

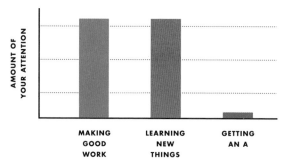

CHAPTER NINE

GRADES

When we talk about how failing is valuable, this of course brings up the question of grades: How are you graded on having useful failures? Are they an F? An A? And really, what about grades in general? What's a "good" GPA? What kind of grades should you be trying to get?

Well, here's the thing about grades: they really don't matter (unless they do).

Trying to sum up an entire class experience—all the mistakes you made, all the things you learned, all the stuff you tried, all the research you did, everything that happened all semester—in one simple letter is absolutely ridiculous and totally worthless (with a couple of exceptions I'll explain below). Don't get me wrong: feedback is incredibly important and totally necessary, and learning how to receive feedback is one of the main points of being at design school to start with, rather than just locking yourself in a room and making stuff by yourself. You should be getting constant feedback from your teacher and your classmates during critiques, during reviews, pretty much every time you're in the class. Receiving feedback is a constant and ongoing process that ideally will happen every single day.

If you are being given constant feedback on your work, you should know where you stand at any given time during the semester and the grade you get on any project should never be a surprise. If the grade you get at the end of the semester is not something you were expecting, then one of two things is happening: first, you might not be paying attention to your critiques and reviews. If you think you're doing A level work and you end up with a D for the class, the problem might be your understanding of what is happening with your work. You might not be paying enough attention to what is going on during conversations about your work. You might be delusional about what you're really doing every day. You might be choosing not to really accept and learn from the feedback you're getting. Second, it could be the fault of your teacher for not explaining the expectations of the class. Your teacher needs to make sure you understand what they are grading you on and how you are being evaluated.

A single letter grade just doesn't give you that much information about how the people who are teaching you feel you are doing in a class. Within art and design school there are very few hard facts and an enormous number of opinions. Opinions from people who know what they're talking about, opinions of people who have generally practiced in the field they are teaching in. Opinions of people who know how to teach art and design. This is to say, these are good opinions—opinions that are valuable and should be listened to but are nonetheless still opinions. "Correct" and "incorrect" don't really exist very often at design school, so real quantitative data that can be calculated into a grade is hard to come by. This is why it is so critically important that your teachers make it very clear to you how they are evaluating you on any given project. That doesn't mean they want you to do it the way they tell you to, however—just that a defined expectation should be communicated.

So when do grades matter? Grades are mostly a function of the practical mechanics of education; they matter when it comes to things like scholarships, getting on the dean's list, receiving honors when you graduate, getting into graduate school, and things like that. These things are not irrelevant, but they are not the point of what you're doing at school. The other place grades matter—and maybe matter most of all—is to your parents. The vast majority of students in art and design school are not children of artists and designers. Generally speaking, your parents are going have a very hard time understanding what you're doing on a daily basis, and so a letter grade for a class is something they can under-stand, because they received letter grades when they were in school. I have seen parents sit in on final critiques of students, and I have to tell you: it is not usually good for the student or the parents. The average non-designer parent just does not understand what is happening in a critique. (My advice is to invite your parents to the opening of your senior show, not your final critique.)

Another way that a letter grade is theoretically useful is to convey to the other teachers at the school what kind of student you are. Of course I think this has a lot of problems, for all of the reasons I mentioned above, but it can be useful as a macro view of a student: seeing your grades for past classes can help me as a teacher have a general idea of where you are as a student. Knowing this can help me help you be better. It will let me know that maybe you need a little more help with certain kinds of projects. It will give me a very general sense of your strengths and weaknesses. It might help me understand where your interests are if you always get good grades in certain kinds of classes and bad grades in other kinds. It can help me understand where your curiosity lies.

When it comes to grades, here's the thing: do not work for a good grade. Work for making good work. Work for learning something. Work for coming out of a class knowing more stuff than you did when you went in. If this happens to result in an A instead of a B+ that's fine, but if all you're doing is trying to get an A, then you will most likely do what you think the teacher wants you to do. Just focusing on making the teacher happy is not what you are at school for. You are not there to impress your teachers; you are there to impress yourself. You are there to grow and evolve. You are there for what I call "holy shit!" moments, when suddenly something clicks and you see the world in a different way than you did a minute ago. These moments happen maybe once or twice a semester, but they are incredibly important and they will literally change who you are and shape how you make work. Just working to make a teacher happy does not result in a whole lot of these moments, if any. Sure, you might get an A, but what did you get out of the class?

FOR TEACHERS, grading is simply a reality of being an educator, and almost always the thing I hear teachers say they dislike the most about being a teacher (other than faculty meetings). Personally, I hate grading, but I have found that the following strategy has helped enormously: you must have very clear goals that show the student how their work will be evaluated. For each project sheet, I lay out what I think the goals of the project are and therefore what students will be evaluated against. This way grades become more of a quantitative measurement than simply your professional opinion about the project as a whole.

I often have students grade themselves, using the exact same evaluation criteria that I would use. I have done this both electronically (using online forms) and with a handout, but either way I list the evaluation criteria and leave a space for them to give themselves a score of one to ten. I prefer numbers instead of letters because a letter grade has an emotional connotation burned into students' minds from their past dozen years of primary education. A number is more abstract and therefore more likely to be accurate. I have used self-grading to assign a final grade. I have found that the vast majority of students grade themselves fairly accurately. I was initially worried everyone would give themselves an A for every project, and that did not happen. Quite the opposite—if anything, most students grade themselves lower than I would have. Because of this, I explain to the students that I retain the right to override the grades they give themselves, both high and low. If they did great work but gave themselves a low number, I change it to the higher number, and vice versa for bad work with a high number. I also make it extremely clear to the students that I want them to be completely honest with both themselves and with me about how they think they did. I make sure they understand this is not some clever mind game where they should try to guess what they think I would give them—what matters is what they give themselves.

Over the years what grading students has really taught me is this: students want real grades that reflect what they really did with their projects. One would think that students just want to get an A on every single project regardless of the quality. It turns out they don't want that at all. What they want is a real evaluation of their work, and if the work is bad, they want a grade that reflects that. They do not want an easy A. They want to be called on their bullshit, and they want to be held accountable. This, of course, makes perfect sense—students are in college to learn, and eventually to become part of a professional discipline, and they really want know if they are getting where they need to with their work. The students that do just want the easy A tend to be dilettantes, but the students that are really in it want real, direct, honest evaluations, even if that means bad grades.

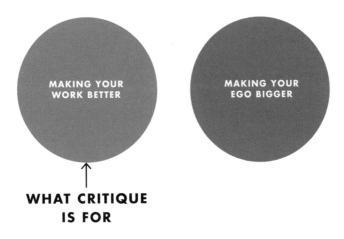

CHAPTER TEN

THE CRITIQUE

This is the longest chapter in this book for a good reason: as a design student, the most fundamental thing you will do together with your classmates and teachers is engage in critique. Critique is one of the most valuable aspects of a formal art and design education. It is also one of the most difficult aspects of the art and design school experience, especially for new students, which is why I have lots to say on the matter.

Critique is a collaborative activity that takes quite a bit of time to learn, both in terms of how to give feedback and how to accept feedback. It is incredibly important to understand that the purpose and value of a critique is to improve the work; critique serves the work, not the person who made the work. A critique of your work is not a critique of your humanity, and making bad work does not make you a bad person. Most of you will read this sentence and say to yourselves, "Oh, of course it is about the work and not about me, I know that," but the reality is that this is an extremely difficult distinction to make when you are standing in front of fifteen people judging what you put up on the wall.

Before you start, there are a few things you need to be aware of when it comes to college-level critiques. First, as a participant in a critique, you should know why you are getting or giving a critique. Some critiques are for exploring concepts, some are for finessing details, some are not even critiques at all but are really celebrations at the end of a project. A critique should have goals; therefore, you should know why the instructor is holding a critique and what the point of the critique is. Sometimes group critiques can turn into performance art, where a few people usually do most of the talking. Ask your instructors to mix up critique formats to avoid this—changing to small groups, one-on-one, "speed-date," written, or online, all can be valuable and will let you hear more voices.

Many people will disagree with me on this next bit, but I do not accept the practice of harsh critiques. You should not get torn apart in a critique. Critiques should not be brutal; critiques should be honest and useful. If you walk away feeling like garbage or like you were beaten up, it was not a useful critique. It was a belittling one. You should walk away from getting a critique feeling empowered and excited to make the work better, not defeated and miserable from the experience.

It is up to both the givers and the receivers of the critique to make this happen.

Last, remember that a critique is not a competition; nobody wins the critique. Everybody is there to learn and grow, and often you can learn as much from giving a critique as you can from getting one. This is why you should always pay close attention to critiques of work by other students, as there is much to be learned from discussing work beyond your own.

GETTING A CRITIQUE

As the person receiving a critique, you have a lot of responsibility for making the process valuable; it is not just putting your work up and saying, "What do you think?" Make sure that you are prepared to ask pointed, specific questions about your work. You should know what you want answers to and be able to clearly ask questions that will get you those answers.

I see very few students doing this, but it is incredibly useful: take notes during your critique! Or, ask someone to take notes for you. Or, ask if it is okay with everybody to record the conversation with your phone's voice memos app if you don't like writing. You should be getting a lot of information thrown at you, and you will need to parse it out and think about what everybody said after the critique is over. In the moment you will often think when someone makes a great point that of course you will remember it, but you will forget the vast majority of what has been said unless you capture it. You are in a convivial, collaborative environment at design school, so you should not be afraid to ask someone to take notes for you.

This next point is too often left unsaid: since you are going to get a lot of opinions about your work, you will have to decide what feedback you do and do not care about. Just because someone tells you something does not mean you have to act on it (this includes your instructor, regardless of what they may say). Everything is up for interpretation, and remember, it is your work, not their work, so you have to decide what matters. That being said, ignoring what everybody says all the time probably won't help your work improve.

It is important to understand that different people react differently to different kinds of critiques, which is why if you are not getting what you need from big group critiques, or one-on-one critiques with your instructor, you should ask for more feedback from your classmates or friends. As a student you need to learn to pull what you need instead of waiting for what you need to be pushed onto you. Design school is about being active, not being passive. If you need more, it is up to you to find it. Ask for help and feedback from as many people as you can, in and out of the class. Sometimes having someone who is not a part of the class give you a read on a project is incredibly helpful.

Usually, the hardest thing about critique is that you have to accept critique without taking it personally, without getting heated, and without getting defensive. You have to approach the critique process as if the feedback you are being given is real and truthful, and not as if it is a personal attack. As I mentioned above, this is very difficult to do (especially in front of a bunch of your peers), and it takes a lot of practice.

GIVING A CRITIQUE

The most important thing about giving someone a critique is that you should always be kind instead of nice. A nice critique is telling someone their work is pretty good just to avoid hurting their feelings. The reality is that a nice critique is much more about not feeling awkward than whether the work is good or not. It is not about helping the work become better, which is the entire point of critique. A kind critique is telling someone their work is not where it needs to be, so they know it needs to be improved or refined. As the critic, it is your responsibility to be kind and honest instead of nice and disingenuous. It is also your responsibility to make sure that your feedback is not derogatory, insulting, or dismissive of the person in front of you. Remember that giving a good critique has absolutely nothing to do with being mean and absolutely everything to do with being helpful and useful.

For those giving feedback, try to avoid giving corrective critiques, comments like "I would do it like this" or "You should try it like that." This might seem like the opposite of most of the critiques you have had. After all, if someone does not tell you the "right" way to do something, how do you do it correctly? Here is the catch: the work is not about how someone else would do it, it is about how you would do it. The main problem with corrective critiques is they often lead to a direct implementation of that comment, and that is not the point of critique. Too often when another student (and especially when a teacher) says "You should do it like this," the student will instantly do exactly that, without much consideration for its validity in their particular project or process.

While there is a bit more relevance in corrective critique for entry-level students who are learning the fundamentals of their profession, it should be done sparingly. The catch here is that it becomes very, very easy for students to develop a habit of relying on critiques to tell them exactly what to do next rather than developing their own exploratory process. A lot of art and design education is about trying stuff until you figure out what works, and being prescribed the exact "right" answer does not let this happen. With this in mind, think of these kinds of discussions as group brainstorming rather than critique. Having everyone bounce ideas off each other (especially at the start of a project) can be useful, as long as you do not rely on waiting for other people's ideas for your project.

What happens when you are not sure what to tell someone who is asking you for feedback? A good place to start is by simply describing what you see. Telling the creator of the work what you are seeing can be very useful; for in-progress work, it is often different from what they intended to show you. Telling them what you think they are trying to say will help them understand what the work is actually saying. This is typically far more valuable than "Do it like this." Another good place to start is by telling the person getting the critique how the work makes you feel. When you look at the work, do you feel excited? Confused? Bored? Angry? Calm? Happy? Sad? Regardless of whether the piece is "art" or "design," your emotional response to it is valid feedback, and it can help the creator of the work create something more meaningful.

FOR TEACHERS, the point of critique is very simple: to help students improve their work. Nothing else matters— not the schedule, not what critiques are supposed to look like, not what you did when you were in school. One of the most important things you can do as a teacher is to mix up how you critique your students. Don't run the exact same critique the exact same way over and over again every week until the semester is over. That is an excellent way to guarantee that your students will start paying less and less attention. I think the archetypal "whole class together in a room, everyone pins up their work and we go around one by one" big-group critique for three straight hours is actually something that should be used sparingly, even though this was exactly how most of my critiques went when I was in school. I usually save the big-group critique for just the first and last critiques of a project. All of the other critiques break away from the big-group critique model.

I do this for a lot of different reasons. The first is that it is quite simply easier to pay attention if you have a small group of five people giving a critique for an hour versus a big group of fifteen people giving a critique for three hours. By the time the fifteenth person presents, everybody has had enough, and those last couple of people inevitably get the short end of the stick. In a three-hour class, I will often split everyone up into three smaller groups, with each group coming in at a specific time to sit with me during the critique. When they are not in their group, they can do whatever they want; they do not have to sit in the classroom and pretend to pay attention. Now this sounds great, but it comes with an understanding: I make sure my students know that when it is time for their group, they need to be on the ball, fully prepared and ready to speak. Nobody just sits quietly when it is only five people talking—everybody must participate fully and contribute to the conversation.

IT ISN'T ABOUT
HARSH CRITIQUES.
IT ISN'T ABOUT
CRITIQUES THAT TEAR
YOUR WORK APART.

AND IT ISN'T ABOUT
EASY CRITIQUES.
IT ISN'T ABOUT
CRITIQUES THAT
FEED YOUR EGO.

IT'S ABOUT
USEFUL CRITIQUES.

The second reason I like to avoid big-group critiques is that I prefer to put the ownership of the critique on the students, not on me. Sometimes I'll have those three separate groups come in all at the same time, sit in different parts of the classroom, and give each other feedback. I do this intentionally because it is not physically possible for me to be in three places at once; therefore, the students learn how to take charge of their own critique. The students have more ownership when they critique each other; they tend to really listen to what their classmates say about the work instead of just waiting for me to tell them exactly what to do. The logical counterargument to this is that I, as the teacher, know more stuff, and therefore my critique is more valid and useful than that of their fellow students. I fully reject this idea, because I think that you learn at least as much, and maybe more, by giving critique as you do by receiving critique. With me not in the equation, students always tend to talk more and be more honest with each other, and it ends up being a much more valuable critique. Additionally, it is not as if I am never talking to the students about their work—I talk to them about their work constantly, so they still get more than enough Mitch during the semester.

The third reason I like to avoid big-group critique is that, as mentioned above, it so often becomes performance art. The social dynamics of having fifteen or twenty people in a room together in a big discussion can get dicey. You have unquestionably seen this: the same three or four students do 75 percent of the talking during every single full-group discussion. I absolutely love having students who won't shut up, especially when what they're saying is interesting, insightful, and useful. What I don't love is having the three students who won't shut up overpower the other twelve students — and the more outgoing and confident (sometimes arrogant) students cannot help but be louder and more vocal. Some students — and often more than just one or two — will never speak in a big group critique unless I call on them and force them to. I understand why — some students have social anxiety, which can be severe and debilitating; some students speak English as a second language and are not comfortable with everyone staring at them; some students simply get embarrassed in a big group but are great with just a few people. This obviously does not mean that what these students have to say is not valuable; in fact, what they have to say might be especially valuable because they spend a lot more time thinking instead of speaking.

With all this in mind I use quite a few different modes of critique. All of the techniques I am about to present share one thing in common: I always display a set of questions, things to point out, and things to pay attention to in each critique. "Tell the other person what you think" is not helpful direction, but a really clear list of things to discuss is very helpful. (I will usually show these on the projector or television so everyone can see easily.)

As mentioned above, the first critique format is small groups—I find that the ideal group size is about five or six students. With less than that it can be hard to get the momentum of a discussion going, more than that and students start to act like they do in a big group, with the same couple of people doing most of the talking. Typically, I will have the same groups of students across multiple critique sessions and rotate the time each group comes to class to keep it equitable in terms of who gets a little more sleep. Other times, I will have all the groups in class at the same time meeting in different areas of the classroom. During these critiques—and I tell the students this before we start—I tend to do as little speaking as possible, and preferably I will say nothing at all. I gently and quietly wander around from group to group, just listening and being there if the students need me, which they almost never do.

Another technique, and probably my favorite, is the "speed date" critique. It works exactly like its namesake: I separate students into two groups. The first group sits around the classroom evenly and then I pair each student in the first group with a student in the second group. Each pair of students will critique each other for approximately ten to twelve minutes, and then the students from group two will get up, move over one seat, and repeat the process. I tell the students that they should each critique the other's work for half the time and then switch, and I encourage them to keep talking to each other no matter what, even if they are done giving each other feedback. They can talk about literally anything they want, but I do not want them just sitting there staring at each other. I usually do six rounds of critique using this method.

This process does a lot of things, and I say all of the following to the students before we start: I have found that students tend to learn as much (or more) from explaining their work six times as they do from getting six different sets of feedback. Having to think about, process, and verbalize what they are doing six times helps them really understand what they are trying to accomplish with the project. This technique also forces students to reconcile six sets of feedback and then decide what is important; if all six people say the same thing, that might be worth paying serious attention to. I also love that this forces the students who never talk to engage in dialogue about their work. I understand that for some students this process is truly frightening, but as designers they will have no choice but to speak with clients, with other employees, and with their bosses about what they are up to, so this is a safe and supportive place to learn how to do that. I emphasize that this is not about whether they like the person they're paired up with—that person might be someone they are not fond of (or even an ex-romantic partner)—but it doesn't matter, as this is about the work and these conversations have to serve the work. The good news is that if they hate the person across from them, in twelve minutes they will have a new partner.

The last kind of critique I like to run is a written, silent critique. There are lots of ways to do this, both in person and online. For in-person, I have students spread out or pin up their work and then I give everybody a stack of Post-it notes. I ask them to reference the questions I have posted and then go around piece by piece, write down their feedback, and stick it to the work. Alternatively, this can be done online with digital objects pretty easily, using any sort of shared document platform that allows for commenting. I don't know what technology is going to be around when you're reading this book, but as of 2023 I use Dropbox Paper, Discord, Figma, or even Google Docs—whatever works is fine, as this is not about the technology at all, it is about the feedback. This process can get to be a little bit overwhelming if every single student has to leave written notes for every single other student, so in a class larger than ten students I will ask them all to give feedback to the eight students to the right of where their own work is pinned up or laid out.

Something else to be aware of is that all of these critiques are extremely tiring for the students, as they really have to focus on speaking and participating rather than just waiting for me to talk. Often the students are going to be talking and thinking with a lot more intensity than in other classes, so do not be afraid to end the class after these critiques; students can always talk to you one-on-one as needed.

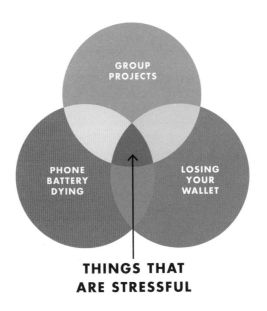

**THINGS THAT
ARE STRESSFUL**

CHAPTER ELEVEN

COLLABORATION

The way students react to a group project assignment has always amused me. There are always some groans and some exasperated sighs, their eyes get wide, they awkwardly shift in their seats, and you can tell they are uncomfortable—very uncomfortable—with the idea of doing a group project. Even the people who like doing group projects get uncomfortable when I first mention it.

Here is the thing: design is a collaborative activity. Both in and out of school you are and will always be working with other people and collaborating on making work. Even if you are locked alone in a room creating work, you are still collaborating with a client or with the client's audience.

Therefore, design school itself is a group project. I guarantee that you will be working side by side with your classmates and your teachers in creating work, critiquing work, generating ideas, experimenting, learning, trying

stuff out, and all the other things you will do during
school. Everything you do is a group project, even work
you think you are doing alone. With this in mind it is
really important that you learn to have a convivial
attitude. You need to learn to play well with others.
I know how incredibly difficult this is for some students.
Some of them just don't get along that well with other
people. Some have severe, crippling social anxiety. Some
of them are so full of themselves that they don't care
what anybody else has to say. And the group dynamic
can be brutal: What if you get assigned to a group with
someone who did something rude to you in high school?
Or someone you know treated a friend badly? What if
you are put in a group with someone you know is lazy,
and you know they are going to blow off the assignment?
What if you get put in a group with someone you simply
hate? Then there is the matter of asserting yourself within
the group; this is very easy for some and incredibly hard
for others. Simply being heard can be a huge hurdle.

I say this exact sentence to my students every time
I give a group project: "Are you freaking out about
working in a group? Get over it. Work the project."
I absolutely, positively, guarantee that when you start
working professionally, you will have no choice but to
work with people you don't like. You probably won't
dislike everyone, but you will absolutely not like someone
you have to deal with regularly. Collaboration is an
important part of life as a designer. You have to learn

how to do it, and I very strongly suggest you learn how to do it well. Someone who is good at working collaboratively is someone who will be invited to do more complex projects and who will be asked to work on larger, high-profile projects. Working well with others will only help your career; working poorly with others will likely hurt it.

I can distinctly remember an upper-level class I taught where, at the beginning of the semester, I mentioned there would be a group project coming up. Over the next week, I had three different students come to me privately and tell me that they would not work with someone in the class—and all three of them pointed to the same person. Think about that for a moment: three out of fifteen students all singled out the same person as a problem—twenty percent of the class did not want anything to do with this individual.

The student that everybody was talking about was (I thought) an excellent designer, and I had always been impressed with their work. Unfortunately, the other students felt that they were horrible to deal with inter-personally, they were very arrogant and unwilling to listen to others, and they offered no flexibility or consideration for other ideas. They quite simply did not care about—and did not want to consider caring about—what their classmates had to say about a project. These are the kind of personality traits that will eventually get you fired from a job; nobody will ever want to work with a person like that if they don't have to. Later on, I spoke with that person privately and explained that their classmates did not want to work with them. That student—while understandably upset and hurt—was also glad to know that this was such a big problem and worked to change how they dealt with other people.

The good news is that school is an excellent place to hone your skills at working in groups, and you will have a lot of opportunities to practice. The overarching rule for working in groups is quite simple: serve the project, not your ego. You do not put your ego first. You do not put the need to be right first. You do not put the need to have your idea be the one your group chooses first. You have to put your project itself first; as a group you need to come together and figure out what will best serve the needs of the project, regardless of who the idea came from, who talked the most, or anything else outside of the actual project. Working in groups is about empathy and consideration—empathy for the other group members' perspectives and consideration of their ideas.

Here is the other thing: you liking the people in your group is absolutely and completely irrelevant. It quite simply does not matter whether the people in your group are your friends or your enemies, whether you like or dislike their work, or whether they are good or bad students. This does not matter, and letting stuff like this matter is what makes groups fall apart. Allowing interpersonal bullshit to get in front of the needs of the project is what makes a bad group project a bad group project. As you read this now, it makes perfect sense, right? Obviously, everyone needs to work together to make a great project, but it becomes much more difficult in the actual situation of dealing with your classmates on something that all of you want to do well on and that you all care about (or at least should care about).

In every context where you are with other people there are different personalities—some people are outgoing, some people are quiet and reserved, some people are very improvisational and off the cuff, some people are very thoughtful and introspective. These are not problems with working in a group, this is what is *great* about working in a group: getting to collaborate with people who are not you. This is how you learn to be empathetic and considerate of other perspectives, and how you become a much, much better designer.

Beyond group projects, I have always found that as a student I learn at least as much from my classmates as I do from my teachers. Learning does not only happen in the formal context of a critique inside the classroom. In fact, I think the best learning happens very organically and very naturally, just by being in the same physical space as your classmates. This is why if you are in a program that gives you a studio space on campus, you should use that space as much as you possibly can. Do not take your work home at the end of the day to do everything alone in your dorm room or your apartment (unless you absolutely have to). Take the opportunity to work side by side with the other students, because the casual, unplanned "Hey, what do you think about this?" conversations that happen in studio after class are absolutely invaluable. This is the kind of interaction you quite simply cannot get by taking a class on YouTube or online. When you approach doing work in the studio not as "These people are going to annoy me while I am trying to get my stuff done" and instead as "These people can look at what I am doing while I am doing it and offer some thoughts," the value of that time together outside of class makes a lot more sense.

FOR TEACHERS, this is really pretty simple: give group projects and make students work together. I will add that when doing so, hold the students accountable and explain very clearly that at the end of the project, the students will be doing a written evaluation of their teammates. Each member of the group is given a place (usually a Google form) to grade every other member of the group on things like commitment, willingness to listen to others, idea and concept generation, and general collaborative attitude, and there is also room for comments. This way if a student blows off the project, is horrible to deal with, doesn't come up with any ideas, or barely contributes to the project, their teammates will be able to let me know, and that student will be called on it. I collect the evaluations and then give the students anonymous data based on what their teammates said about them. They must understand that the point here is not that person X does not like them but that they need to work on these specific things to get better at collaborating. This makes doing a group project valuable both in terms of working together on something interesting and in terms of learning how to work together in a group.

Something else I do that is a little more subtle but I think equally important: I encourage students to talk to each other during class when they are not actively engaged in another activity. If I'm busy giving critique to a small group of students, I want any other students that are in the room to talk to each other. They do not have to sit there quietly waiting for their turn; I would much rather they engage in dialogue with their classmates. While this can make the room louder and more chaotic, I think the trade-off is well worth it. Instead of students just sitting with their headphones on and their heads down, they're actually talking and learning and discovering things together. They may not even be talking about the project in front of them, but I still think it is important to talk to each other, even if it is about music or movies or whatever. The act of engaging with other people who are in front of them is something that students need to do as often as possible, instead of withdrawing into social media or text messages.

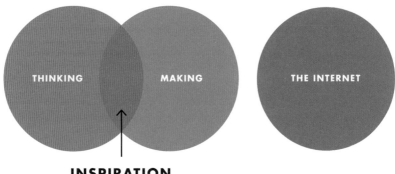

CHAPTER TWELVE

INSPIRATION

There is an enormous amount of stuff written about design available to everyone. There are lots and lots and lots of books, magazines, essays, blogs, and even podcasts and documentaries. Virtually every college has a library, and in that library will be a section of books about art and design. You will be given reading assignments by the teachers in most of your classes, especially the classes dealing with art and design history. There is also a preponderance of visual information out there, especially on the Internet. Endless social media posts, online magazines, blogs, essays, videos—the list goes on. There is no shortage of stuff to read about.

Designers—especially students and young designers—have a tendency to constantly look at examples of design, read stuff written about design, listen to other designers talk about their design work, and generally consume as much design content as they can.

They often do this in the name of inspiration—they need to get an idea for a project and are not sure what to do, so they look at how other designers did a similar project and hope to get inspired. There is an enormous, toxic problem with this: they are looking at pre-thought ideas. They are seeing how somebody else already figured out how to make the thing that they are supposed to be making themselves. In the name of inspiration what they are really doing is filling out a template for a project. They are not really designing, they are not inventing, they are not developing fresh new approaches to something—they are duplicating how somebody else did it first. They are taking a shortcut to somebody else's idea for how to complete a project.

What's the point of doing this? What are you really learning about other than how to be really good at using the Internet to find design stuff or knowing what are the best social media accounts to follow for looking at cool, trendy work? Design education, especially at the very starting levels, involves an element of imitation and studying how "the masters" did it before you. There's a lot of value to taking an existing design, breaking it apart, analyzing it, and really understanding why decisions were made the way they were made, how the designer came up with the final outcome of a project, and how the process affected the outcomes. You are trying to understand the creative process by really diving deep into how someone else did it, so you can start to understand how to make decisions in your own work. I maintain this part of process has nothing to do with inspiration. This is about learning and education.

However, "I don't know what to do for this project so I'll go look at how other designers did it first and get inspired" is not about learning and education. It is in fact the exact opposite. It is the least interesting, least revealing, least valuable way to get to the end of a project. In my classes, for almost every single project I assign, more than one student will ask if I can show them how other students from previous semesters did the same project. My answer is always a quick and definitive "absolutely not." I have never done it, and I will never do it. I don't care (and they should not care) how students three years ago did the project. I care about (and they should care about) how a student standing in front of me does the project right now.

This of course leads to a very legitimate question: "How do I get inspired?" Inspiration and ideas don't come from the outside, they come from the inside. They come from within the mind of a designer and are a synthesis of all of their ideas and experiences. When a designer just Googles to see how other people would do the same project, this internal synthesis is interrupted by seeing a final outcome. This person does not have that chance to let stuff ferment in their brain and transform and translate it into something new and interesting. It just becomes something they try to duplicate. I really don't believe in "inspiration." I believe in process. I believe in making things, I believe in trying stuff, seeing what happens, and then trying new stuff based on what did and did not work. I have learned definitively and without question that making makes ideas.

The biggest irony here is that the best books (and essays, and websites, etcetera) about "design" are not books about design. They are books about everything else. As a creative practitioner you need to fuel your mind with interesting things, and you need to keep refueling. This is why I strongly encourage (and require) students to look at stuff that is not "design." I want them to look at movies, I want them to look at art, I want them to listen to music, I want them to take a walk outside, I want them to socialize with their friends. All of this stuff feeds design far better and far more usefully than just Googling how another designer did something. The more of the world you have inside your mind, the more context and visual language you have to express your ideas. The more things you've seen, the more stuff you've experienced —all of these things add up to a much larger vocabulary in your head when it comes to making stuff. If the only stuff you look at is design—especially design in your field of study—the only vocabulary you have is a homogenized, predictable design language that has been pre-thought and pre–figured out way before you even got there. This makes it very difficult to think laterally and hit on unique, unexpected, and interesting ideas for your work.

"But I'm stuck and I have no idea what to do for this project. What should I do?" I have heard this question over and over from my students (and from professional designers). My advice is always the same. I look that student in the eye, and with a little grin on my face, I say, "Just shut up and make something." I explain that they do not have to make something good. They don't have to make something interesting. They don't even have to make something that is directly related to the assignment. All they have to do is stop talking, stop overthinking, stop worrying, stop panicking, and just make something. Something that nobody else ever has to see. They can make the worst thing that has ever been made in the history of art and design. That is fine, as long as they make something, and from making something they will get ideas. This always works.

And that is what I call inspiration.

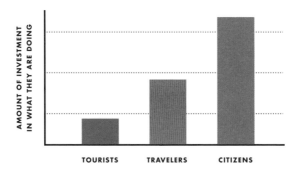

CHAPTER THIRTEEN

TOURISTS, TRAVELERS, AND CITIZENS

In addition to all of the required studio courses you will take as part of completing your degree, you will have to take a number of classes outside of your major. You will have elective studio classes—some of which you will get to choose, some that may be chosen for you. You will also have a number of required liberal arts and general education classes, and hopefully you will have some history classes: in the history of art and also specific to your major. There is a tendency among design students to treat these classes—especially liberal arts, history, and general education classes—like they do not care about them very much. Often students will do just enough to get by and not really worry about too much other than squeezing out a good grade. This is a missed opportunity, and I explain how students approach both non-major and major classes by using three categories: you can be a *tourist*, you can be a *traveler*, or you can be a *citizen*.

When tourists visit someplace new, they approach it in a safe and detached way. First, they want to see the "sights"—all of the things that every other tourist wants to see—the big landmarks, the popular spots, the places with tons of people in line to see the same thing that every other tourist has seen. They want to see and experience things that have been made comfortable for people who are not local. Yes, what they want to experience may be a legitimate part of the culture of the country or city they are visiting, but it is culture that has been sanitized and made safe and palatable for tourists. Tourists like to be comfortable and have everything laid out for them on a simple map that they can follow around town. They don't really want to discover new stuff for themselves, they want to be told what the cool stuff is and then see it in an unchallenging, predictable way with all of the other tourists. Tourists want to see the very top part of the iceberg sticking out of the water —they have no interest in diving deeper. They want the "greatest hits" of a place, not to discover anything deeper.

Travelers, on the other hand, want something more "real." They want to truly experience the culture, the people, the food, the life of a new place. They are interested in going off the beaten path. They do not just want to hit all the tourist hot spots. Travelers want to really understand what life is like in this new place—

they want to eat what and where the people who live there eat, and they want to spend time doing the things the people who live there spend time doing. A traveler explores a new city more on instinct and chance then on the preplanned tourist guides that are available at the airport. A traveler wants to be a local, even if only for a short time. Therefore, travelers treat a new place with more respect and compassion than tourists do—they understand that there are good, tourist-friendly parts of every city, but also "bad" parts too, places where tourists are not meant to go, and that inside of these places some really interesting, authentic, and real things can happen. Travelers want to explore a new place, and they are willing to be flexible and change plans on a whim if they hear about something interesting happening elsewhere. Travelers treat a destination like it is a place that real people live, not just a place that people visit.

Citizens are the people who live in a place. They have full ownership of this place—it is their city or town and the place they call home. This is where they make their living, where many of their friends are, and where they settle in at night. They have an intimate and detailed knowledge of everything about where they live: the best places to eat, the best parks to visit, the coolest places to see—they know it all. They have seen where this place was and where it is now, and they have ideas about where it is going. Citizens know the places to go that are worth your time and the other places that are just for the tourists. They understand the good and bad of where they live. They are fluent in this place, not just in terms of the language, but in terms of culture—they understand all of the local culture, because they are a part of the culture.

For each class you take, you will need to decide: Are you a tourist, a traveler, or a citizen? You can think about how tourists, travelers, and citizens experience a place the same way students at design school experience their classes. There's nothing wrong with any of these options; each kind of person simply wants different things out of a visit to a new place—the same way you will have different expectations and desires for every class you take, major studio or otherwise. You are not going to love every class you take at design school—and that will include your required, major classes. But it is very important that you are a citizen of the major you're in; you need to have full ownership over the curriculum and what you are learning. And, just as you may not like every single part of the city you are a citizen of, you may not like and enjoy every class you take in your major. However, as a citizen of your discipline you do need to own your major, to give it a proper amount of attention and to actively understand what is happening in every one of these classes, the same way citizens pay attention to what is happening around them in their city, because it directly affects them. Casually skimming through a class like a tourist means you will get a lot less out of it than if you acted like a traveler and really explored the topic.

EVEN A CLASS
OR A PROJECT
THAT YOU HATE
CAN STILL BE
WORTHWHILE:
IT CAN TEACH
YOU WHAT KIND
OF WORK YOU
DON'T WANT
TO DO.

This doesn't mean you need to be a citizen of every single class you take. As a design student you will have such an intense load of classes, projects, events, sports, clubs, etcetera, all vying for attention, that being a citizen of every single thing you do in a semester is nearly impossible. You will need to decide which classes in a given semester deserve more or less attention than the others. As a teacher I always want to think that whatever class I am teaching is clearly the most important class that each student is taking, but that is rarely true. Students who are honest with themselves and their teachers about what they want out of a given class, rather than pretending to care when they clearly don't, are much more respectful to both the class and the teacher.

The cool thing about being a tourist or a traveler is that you might take a class you were not planning on being that excited about, that turns out to have a profound effect on your work. You can then come back to that topic or idea as a citizen: maybe you do a minor or concentration in that discipline, or even a double major, or possibly focus on it in graduate school. The same way a tourist can visit a country that has a profound effect on their life, a student can take a class in another discipline that has a profound effect on their work. One of the best things about design school is that you have an opportunity to visit lots and lots of different disciplines and then decide if any of them are really important to you. You are allowed to take one class or do an entire other major in something you find really interesting. This is something you need to take advantage of as a student: you should take lots of different classes on lots of different topics and treat them all seriously. Yes, you want to find out what you like, but it is equally valuable to find out what you don't like.

**THINGS THAT NEED
YOUR ATTENTION**

CHAPTER FOURTEEN

ORGANIZATION

Generally speaking, as an undergraduate design student doing a BFA, you will take five classes a semester. Two of those classes are usually general education or liberal arts classes, such as history, physics, or writing. These are all very important classes but are not project-based design studios. The other three classes are studio classes where you are making stuff and working a lot of hours outside of class trying to get everything done. (If you are doing a BA, generally it is reversed: two classes a semester are studio classes and three are not.) In an average studio class, you will probably make three to five projects in a semester. Multiply that by three studio classes, and you will be making as many as nine to fifteen projects in a fifteen-week-long semester. This is an enormous amount of stuff to pay attention to and keep track of, and that does not include all of your other classes, papers, exams, and so on. Once you graduate and get a job as a designer, you will probably not work on three or four completely separate projects a month from start to finish—your classes are a lot of work.

You need to remember that college is not just about academics; you should also be trying to have some fun. You should be meeting new people, exploring the city or town where your college is, doing things outside of studios and classes. Most people make lifelong friends while they are in college, and you don't get to do this by only paying attention to your classes and nothing else. I contend that the social part of college is at least as important as the academic. Oh, and let's not forget that you have to live. You have to eat, you have to sleep, and you have to clean yourself, your clothes, and your room (hopefully regularly).

During the semester there is a lot happening in a very compressed amount of time, often taking place in shared environments like studios and dormitories. It can get extremely stressful and very, very overwhelming, to say the least. And that's why two things are extremely important, and you may not have thought about them yet: first, you need to be able to organize and keep track of this entire chaotic mess so you don't miss deadlines and social events. Second, you need to know when to completely ignore this entire chaotic mess and just relax and hang out and watch Netflix and not worry about anything at all. A lot of students don't seem to recognize that not only can they take a break, they absolutely need to take a break—and they should probably do this a lot more often than they realize.

How you choose to organize your classes, your projects, and your social agenda doesn't really matter. You can use digital tools like calendars or to-do lists, or physical tools like notebooks or bullet journals— anything goes as long as it works. What does matter is that you are keeping track. It is far too easy to say to yourself, "Oh, I'll remember that" when given a deadline or a goal, only to immediately not remember it as soon as you walk out of the classroom. Design school is considered a professional environment, and as such you are going to be held accountable for getting your assignments done, handing them in on time, and paying attention to details. You have to have some kind of system—no matter what it is. Personally, I use a combination of a calendar application and a simple note-taking application, both of which sync on all of my devices. This allows me to keep track of when things are due and to easily note down things I need to remember. Unfortunately, my handwriting is essentially unreadable, so for me sketchbooks are only for sketching, and digital tools are where I record information I need to remember. I will note that printing out your lists or calendars and pinning them up is an excellent idea. Seeing everything on your dorm room wall at once—what has to get done and when it is due—and, most satisfyingly, being able to cross completed things off your list with a pencil is incredibly helpful and very cathartic. Sounds silly, right? It is fantastic. I highly recommended you try it.

Figuring out a system is good for more than one reason. Once you are able to keep track of everything so that you know you're not missing anything and you don't have to worry about it, you can do the second important thing I mentioned above: relaxing. I cannot stress enough how important it is to just stop once in a while. Yes, you have deadlines. Yes, you have a ton to do. Yes, you have a limited amount of time to do it. But you are also a human being, and you need to take breaks. You need to just sit on the couch and watch movies once in a while. You need to get off campus and go to a concert. You need to take a trip to visit a friend at another college. This all seems obvious, but so many students never take a break—they only stop when the semester ends. This is a toxic habit that will lead to worse work, not better. The importance of fun and relaxation cannot be overstated: it will help you feel better mentally, it will lessen your stress, and it will make your work better when you do get back to it.

FOR TEACHERS, it will help a lot of students to give really clear deadlines that you at least attempt to stick to. We all know that these deadlines frequently shift, but starting out with a solid idea of what will happen over the course of the semester helps students organize themselves quite a bit. On my syllabus I tend to break down the semester into weeks ("Week 4 to Week 7: Project 2"). As I assign each project, I will write out a week-by-week schedule of what to expect for each class meeting during the course of the project. I always clarify that this may change but I'd like to at least start with something solid so students can roughly pencil in the schedule and have a sense of where they're going in my class.

When you are laying out your projects for the semester, consider when assignments in other classes will be due and think about shifting some deadlines so students do not have three projects due in the same couple of days. This is something that would be great to discuss in faculty meetings so that everyone teaching has a broad idea of when everyone else is going to have projects due. It is not really possible to coordinate seamlessly with your colleagues, but if you teach sophomores, for example, and you know that the other sophomore classes in your department have a big project due on week seven, make yours due on week six or week eight. In commercial practice you generally do not have three different projects for three different clients all due on the same Tuesday—but in college this is very common.

This next one might be controversial: I almost never make my students sit in class when we have finished what we need to accomplish for the day. Instead, I let them leave. As a student and as an educator, I have seen far too many times when a class is essentially over, but because it has been scheduled until 11:50 A.M., everyone has to sit there and work until 11:50 A.M. I find that strategy completely absurd. It treats students like they are kids (and we know how I feel about that) who have to be watched until the bell rings lest they go out and decide how they want to spend their time. Having said that, I am completely and easily available to any and all students who need me during that extra class time. What usually happens is that the students who don't need to talk to me leave and the students who need some help stay. This is a much, much better way to run a class than to force everyone to sit with their headphones on while the clock runs out. It makes students understand that their time is their own and they need to use it wisely. I also make it clear that since they will likely leave class early, they had better be on the ball while they are there—my students know they need to be prepared and ready to contribute to the class when it starts.

I do not allow for any "extra credit." The projects I assign during the semester are the projects they will be evaluated on. Extra credit is a way to pull something out of your butt to try to make up for bad work, and it is a ridiculous concept, especially in the creative fields. I also rarely allow students to rework a project for a better grade. By the time a project is due, they have had many, many opportunities for feedback, and if the project isn't good when it is due, then it is not going to be good later. Additionally, allowing them to work on something that was already due weeks earlier means that they will be absolutely buried with work during those last few weeks of the semester. If a student wants to redo a project for themselves because they didn't like how it turned out or they want to make changes to include it in their portfolio, I am more than happy to give them as much feedback as they'd like, but the grade they get on the project when it is due is the grade they get on the project.

Last, give your students a day off once in a while. If I have a project due on a Thursday, sometimes I won't introduce the next project until Tuesday, and my students will get the weekend off. I can tell you from experience this is always incredibly appreciated, and I think it results in better work for most of the students throughout the semester. Once again, we need to treat students like the adults they are and trust that they won't forget everything they've learned if they take a few days off from thinking about class. At least a few times a semester I will declare a "work day" when students can come in if they want to and I will be available and happy to talk with them, but if all they need to do is work, they can work. The more you respect students' time, the more you allow students to make their own choices about where to put their effort, the less you hold their hands and babysit them, the quicker they learn to have agency and you-ness.

GETTING A GOOD
NIGHT'S SLEEP

ALL-NIGHTERS

**THINGS THAT
ARE HEROIC**

CHAPTER FIFTEEN

HUMAN FIRST

If you ask most designers about what it was like to
go through school, many will tell you all about the
late nights, the huge workload, the headaches from the
computer screen, all the stress, all the work, and all the
torment of getting through design school. Most designers
wear this like a badge of honor—they made it through
something that was incredibly difficult that most normal
people could never handle. They love this idea that design
school has to be nearly impossible, that you have to put
in the pain and struggle in order to get through it, that
you have to forget about sleeping well, eating well, and
having a social life just so you can work your way
through this nightmarish ordeal and get your degree.

This is one of many toxic myths about design school.
Lucky for you that you're reading this book, so I can tell
you the real secret about making it through design school:
self-care is more important than all of that stuff. We seem

to forget that we are human beings first, designers second, and human beings need to sleep. Human beings need to eat most meals not out of a vending machine at two o'clock in the morning, human beings need to get some basic level of physical exercise, and human beings need to have social interactions with other human beings. These things are not options, they are requirements.

Now, let's talk about the "all-nighter." The all-nighter is considered a rite of passage in many design programs—something that you are going to have to do, maybe often, and then get to brag about a few days later. The reality is that no matter how great your time management is, you will probably have to do some late nights once in a while. This won't change after you leave school, either—if you have a huge deadline at your studio, you will likely have to work some extra hours. I have done quite a few all-nighters, especially when I was studying architecture—a major that is notorious for making students pull all-nighters. I have to be honest: sometimes these were fun, but once 4:00 A.M. hit, things would start getting...weird. Not productive, but weird. I am not denying that there is some social aspect to staying up with a bunch of your classmates—it can be a bonding experience. I fondly remember more than a few 4:00 A.M. trips to the Little Gem Diner in Syracuse, New York, for coffee and breakfast food with a group of my all-nighter architecture friends back in the early 1990s. But here's the thing: *all-nighters are not heroic.*

All-nighters are not something you should hope you get to do all the time. I am always more impressed when a student gets a good night's sleep rather than pounding Red Bulls all night just to finish a project. Most of the time it is much better to get at least a few hours of sleep rather than try to do an all-nighter. The work you make during an all-nighter is almost never as good as work you do when you have slept well.

Most teachers will not tell you this in class, but we all think it is totally okay if you take a day off once in a while for your mental health. You really will feel better physically and mentally if you take an hour away from sitting at the computer a few times a week and instead get a little bit of exercise. Go to the gym, take a walk, shoot some hoops, whatever — but do it offline, not online.

The other thing about design school that is only discussed fleetingly and casually is that it is not just an academic experience. It is also a social experience, and usually one of the most formative social experiences of your life. If the only thing you do is pay attention to your classes and projects, you are missing out on something really important: your development into an adult human being. You should interact socially with others, and do so often. You should have fun. You should make friends, have relationships, and enjoy what is a unique and special time in your life. This does not mean you have to go to a lot of parties, do a lot of drugs and drink a lot of alcohol, or have a lot of casual sex to get the most out of school.

This also does not mean that you have to ignore those things, either. If you are fortunate enough to be able to go to college, then have the full "college experience" as best you can. You are missing out on life-changing events if you don't.

Something that is not uncommon in college is seeing spikes in your anxiety and stress levels. I often see this happen around week four or five of the first semester of college. Suddenly the excitement, the energy, and the amazing newness of everything wears off and you start getting into a little bit of a grind. Those of you living away from home for the first time suddenly get incredibly homesick. You might find that socializing with other people becomes very difficult, and you just want to be left alone and feel comfortable and in control of your surroundings. Your sleep habits might suddenly change dramatically; you might start finding it more difficult to sleep—especially if you live in a dorm with a roommate who does not respect your boundaries. Or you might start sleeping a lot more than usual, and just getting out of bed in the morning (or, let's be honest, in the afternoon) can become a major roadblock. Eating habits may change dramatically, especially with the all-you-can-eat meal plans you have paid for. You may just start feeling (for lack of a better word) shitty all the time.

Please listen to me on this one: what you should not do is nothing. You should not just bury your head in the books and work harder, you should not just accept that you're not sleeping, you should not be miserable and anxious all the time. What you should do is get help. Self-care is realizing you are not feeling good—that you may be starting to spiral downward and that now it is time to reach out to someone. These experiences are incredibly common in college, and the people who run student services at your school know this is going to happen. They are ready for this to happen, and they know how to help you through these periods in your life. That help might be from a mental health professional you know from home who will do a video chat with you. That help may come from your parents or siblings or friends from home, but it must come from somewhere. For many students, college is a completely new, completely alien, completely ridiculous, and completely over-the-top environment, and it can be very difficult to deal with. Help is readily available, and you must be self-aware enough to take advantage of it.

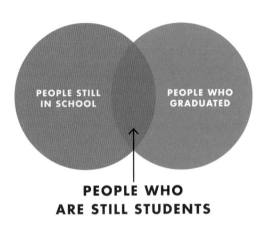

PEOPLE STILL
IN SCHOOL

PEOPLE WHO
GRADUATED

PEOPLE WHO
ARE STILL STUDENTS

CHAPTER SIXTEEN

SCHOOL IS NOT OVER

Congratulations! You just graduated! You have completed many years of learning a profession in an intense, engaging, and exciting way. You met many new people, made a lot of new friends, and created new connections, and you have been exposed to the wonderful world of art and design. You learned how to experiment, make decisions, and develop agency and a strong sense of inquiry and curiosity. You have grown tremendously in four (more or less) years, and now you have been unleashed upon the world. School is over, and now it is time to transition into being a professional designer.

Except as it turns out…school is not over.

School is never over. You never really graduate, and you are never done with your education. The people who are truly in it, the people who are citizens of design, never really graduate. The people who look at commencement as the start of a lifelong creative practice don't stop their education just because they got a cap and gown. Learning is something they do until they die.

On a purely practical level, design is an industry that relies heavily on technology, and as a practitioner of design, you will at a bare minimum need to remain current on software and technology. It might be literally a part of your job description to learn new stuff and at least know the current versions of software and other technologies that will help you do your job. What is far, far more important than just knowing the technology is not becoming stagnant in your practice. You will not want to spend your career just doing what you know how to do already over and over and over again until you retire or die. This is what people who stop learning do: they do what they know and don't know new things. The only way that you will break out of that rather boring path is to keep endlessly learning. As someone who makes things for a living, you owe it to your clients, your employers, and, most important, to yourself to never stop being a student.

I take this idea of "forever a student" very seriously, and I can prove it: after I received tenure at Rochester Institute of Technology, I enrolled in the MFA Furniture Design program there. Furniture, woodworking, and three-dimensional art is something I have always been interested in, and now I have an opportunity to do something about it. As a faculty member at RIT I can take classes for free and only have to pay for materials

IF YOU ONLY
DO STUFF THAT
YOU ALREADY
KNOW HOW
TO DO,
IT'S HARD
TO DISCOVER
NEW STUFF
THAT YOU MIGHT
LOVE TO DO.

and tools. I see this as such an incredible opportunity. I have always said that if I ever hit the lottery, I will spend the rest of my life getting master's degrees, and now I get to do that! As far as I'm concerned, teaching full-time is hitting the lottery, and being able to get another MFA is incredible. This is proving to be interesting in a lot of different ways, not the least of which is being a student after having taught for so long. Not only am I getting to learn a completely new discipline and getting to make interesting furniture and sculptural pieces but I'm also getting to refine and improve how I teach based on my actual experience of being a student again. As an added bonus, I will be able to teach new subjects that I was never qualified to teach before, like 3D foundations, sculpture, and so on.

That sounds great, but how do you keep learning after you leave campus? What if you do not have the opportunities for continued education that I have? It is likely that many of you will not go back to school for another degree. We will talk about graduate school in the next chapter, but most people do not go forward with that—the BFA or BA is all you need to be a professional designer. You are lucky; information has never been easier to access in the history of humanity than it is right now, and there are so, so, so many ways to continue your education. As I mentioned in the introduction of this book, you can access the entire world of knowledge on YouTube and other streaming platforms for free, or for a very inexpensive monthly membership. While watching free or cheap tutorials online may not make you an "expert," it can expose you to a whole bunch of new stuff that you may want to take a deeper dive into elsewhere. It is also worth mentioning that I think online video tutorials may be the *best* way to learn software and the like. I rarely do technical demos in my own classes; I encourage students to learn that stuff online, with me as a resource. Even if you want to learn an entirely new field of digital tools that you have never touched before, video learning is the way to go.

Most colleges offer a continuing education program where you can take one-off classes in a huge variety of subjects. This is great because you don't have to enroll as a full-time student or quit your job, and you don't have to move to a new city just to take a college class. Instead, you can just take a class here and there when something strikes your fancy. These classes can vary widely in price—up to and including very expensive—but you will experience a real, in-person, college-level course that can last as long as an entire semester, depending on the institution. Some schools also offer post-baccalaureate programs, which sit in between an undergraduate degree and a graduate degree. Some of these courses are full-time, but others are part-time, and some are remote. Generally, a post-baccalaureate program ends with a certificate or some kind of formal "you completed this successfully" documentation.

Going to industry conferences—especially in the design profession—is a great way to learn new stuff, meet new people, and hopefully even make some connections that could lead to future work. Most conferences will last from one to three days and will feature lots of different people speaking about their own work as well as other relevant topics. Big conferences have multiple people speaking at once in different places, so there will always be something interesting to watch. Many larger conferences offer on-site workshops, classes, and roundtable discussions, often with the speakers themselves. It is not uncommon for an employer to pay for you to go, since you will ideally learn new stuff that will help you do your job more effectively. This is great news, because the admission to these conferences can be expensive and they often require travel and staying at a hotel.

An added bonus to the official program of the conference, and really my favorite part, is all the time in between the speakers, when everyone is milling around and chatting. Often, especially at mid-size and regional conferences, the person you just saw on stage speaking to five hundred people is also wandering around chatting with attendees. You might be able to have a drink with that design hero of yours after their talk, and that can be priceless. I have learned a tremendous amount just by chatting with interesting people about the work they do and the work they admire.

It is also very much worth your time to learn things outside of design. Just because you are a designer does not mean that's the only thing you are allowed to do. If you think you might want to learn something hands-on, there are many craft schools that offer on-site workshops and classes. Schools like Penland (North Carolina), Haystack (Maine), Peters Valley (New Jersey), and Anderson Ranch (Colorado) are places where you go live for a week or two and learn a new craft like ceramics, woodworking, painting, and so on. These schools are immersive ways to learn something completely outside of your discipline. The catch is that these schools are very expensive, but you will get a really intense, hands-on experience for a week or two. Think of it like a vacation where you learn to do something cool. Most of these schools have opportunities to work as a studio assistant, a member of the kitchen staff, etcetera, for reduced or free tuition.

The danger of stopping the learning process when you graduate is that over time you can forget how to learn—all of those habits of inquiry and curiosity can fade away. It is far too easy, and unfortunately far too common, to become intellectually and creatively stagnant. One of the rewards for learning things is wanting to learn *more* things. Never, ever stop being a student—your education does not end with graduation. There are infinite things to learn, and you should spend the rest of your life trying to grab some of that knowledge.

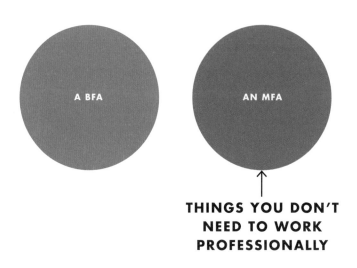

A BFA

AN MFA

THINGS YOU DON'T
NEED TO WORK
PROFESSIONALLY

CHAPTER SEVENTEEN

WHAT ABOUT AN MFA?

A BFA in a design discipline is considered a professional degree, which means it qualifies you to work at the highest possible level of that discipline. Some of the most famous designers only have a BFA; you don't need anything else to work as a professional designer. A BFA should prepare you to start working in an entry-level design position, and from there you can move up all the way to the top of the profession. But what about going beyond your BFA? What about getting a master's degree? Should you be thinking about graduate school before you graduate from your undergrad? Do you need an MFA?

Any good graduate program is a completely different experience than an undergraduate program. The mindset is very distinct from what you did as an undergraduate student: the way the classes are run, how you spend your time, and what the teachers do are all very different from what you did as an undergrad. While you may have classes and assignments and projects given by your teachers, graduate school is generally considered to be a much more independent, self-motivated, and self-oriented experience. Good graduate programs are not just advanced versions of undergraduate programs. You have to think of a master's degree in art and design as a two-year-long independent study rather than as a bunch of classes you have to pass to get a degree.

This difference—which can be quite jarring for those who are not ready for it—is why I very strongly recommend students do not go directly from undergrad into grad. You need at least two to five years of professional experience as a designer before you should be ready to commit to grad school. You need this time to really understand your relationship with design: what you do and do not care about as a designer, what questions you have that you can't seem to answer, what kinds of things you want to spend time on at graduate school. If you go directly from finishing your BFA program in May to starting your MFA in September, you are not going to be ready for the change that is about to come. You will be predisposed to treat it like your fifth year of undergrad, which is a great way to not get much out of grad school.

Graduate school is not class- or project-based; graduate school is inquiry-based. Depending on exactly what courses you enroll in as a graduate student, you will certainly have a chance to learn pragmatic applied techniques and technical stuff, and you can certainly learn how to do things, especially if you are going for an MFA in a different discipline than your BFA. The majority of your time is not spent just being handed assignments that will be due in a few weeks; you will instead be spending a lot more time creating work based on your own ideas and interests, with no formal assignments at all. As a grad student, you will make your own assignments. Graduate school ends in a thesis, which is different from the capstone, degree project, or whatever they call your BFA final project. A graduate thesis is really the subject of another book, but broadly speaking it is you asking a question and then spending two years answering that question, not only by creating design objects but also through a lot of writing and theory. It is not about making a thing, it is about discovering ideas.

With all of that in mind, people go to grad school and get a lot out of the experience. There are three typical reasons why you might decide to get an MFA. The first is because you want to shift your practice into a different discipline. Maybe you have a graphic design BFA but want to shift your practice to painting or furniture design, or you have an industrial design BFA and you want to do more screen-based interactive work. An MFA can be a way to learn a new discipline without having to spend four more years on another BFA. Most graduate programs are two years long, but many schools offer three-year options for people transitioning into an entirely new field, especially for those who do not have art and design related undergraduate degrees. This can make the mix of people who are in a specific grad program very interesting, as you might pursue your MFA next to people with degrees in literature or sociology or engineering or anything else. The perspective they can bring to a grad program can be fascinating and insightful, and it is great to see what happens in a room with such a wide variety of people.

The second reason to get an MFA is to go into teaching art and design full-time. A terminal degree is almost always required to be hired as a full-time educator, and in the arts an MFA is that terminal degree. You can be a part-time teacher (also known as an "adjunct" teacher) with a BFA, but if you want to teach at one school and make a living at it, you will need an MFA. The irony here is that most MFA programs will not actually teach you how to be a teacher, but there are generally opportunities to teach a class or two as a graduate student to get some experience before you try to be hired full-time.

The third reason to get an MFA is simply because you can. If you have the time and money to spend on an MFA, and you want to be back in school for a couple of years, and you can afford not to work, and are able to move to a new place, you can. You can think of this as a gift to yourself: the gift of time to focus on something that isn't work, the gift of curiosity to explore something you've always been curious about, the gift of collaborative conviviality in a place where other people will look at your work, give you feedback, and help you become better.

A graduate school worth attending will be happy to have you come for a visit and have you sit in on some critiques or discussions. They want you to understand what happens there and whether their program is going to work for you. Graduate design programs are like potato chips—they all teach similar topics, but the flavors of each program will vary wildly. The only way you can know if a graduate program is the one for you is to physically go there and see what it is about. You need to see the facilities, you need to see the students and faculty, you need to have a real taste for what actually happens there on a daily basis. The best way to do this is to go there in person and hang out for a day or two. I understand this might not always be possible, but at the very least you need to have multiple conversations with people who either go or have gone to that program—the school will be happy to connect you with current and former students, as well as faculty who can talk to you about their particular flavor of potato chip.

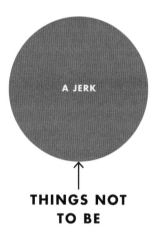

A JERK

↑

**THINGS NOT
TO BE**

CHAPTER EIGHTEEN

REMEMBER YOUR FRIENDS

Here is the worst-kept secret about finding a job in any kind of industry: it helps to know people. A significant percentage of jobs do not come from job postings. They come from a personal connection or relationship. As you start working professionally you will meet more and more people through your job, through social events adjacent to your job, and through conferences or other local and regional design events. You will start to build a network: relationships with people who are aware of what you do for a living and who sometimes can help with jobs, projects, or other things. The good news is that you do not have to graduate before you can start to build your network. In fact, you already have a network — as a designer, your first professional network is the people you are graduating with. You may not think of them this way as you don your cap and gown, but these are the people who will be looking for jobs (just like you), who will hear about positions they don't want or are not qualified for (just like you), and who will get wind of projects or other opportunities they may not be able to take (just like you). Who do you think they would pass these things on to? Who do they know who is also an emerging designer? They know you, that's who.

I am going to pause here and say that you should always treat people well, with respect and kindness, as simply the default for being a good human being, and not just because it might get you a new job or land you a cool project. Be good to other people regardless of who they are, because we could all use more of that in our lives. If someone may not have anything to offer you by way of work, that does not mean you get to be a dick to them. Treat other people well for no other reason than because they are people.

That being said, not being a jerk has other benefits. The thing about the design profession is that opportunities arise all the time. Projects are constantly being passed around to different studios and different independent designers, jobs turn over all the time, and positions open up constantly. Opportunities present themselves every single day. Design is an incredibly small profession; there are a tiny number of people in the world who do this professionally, and the design community is very intertwined. It does not matter what specific discipline of design you are in. If a client has a specific project that their go-to person is not qualified to do, what does that designer do? They do not tell the client, "Sorry, can't help you with that." A smart designer will refer their client to someone they know who can do the project. This makes everyone happy. The client gets the project done without having to hunt around. The designer gets to look good to the client by helping them get the project done. The other designer gets to have a project fall into their lap just because they knew someone.

I say this to all of my seniors right at the start of their last year of school: treat your classmates well, treat them with respect, because you never know who might be your boss or might offer you a job. I have seen classmates get very underhanded and hypercompetitive with each other during senior year. They feel like all of their classmates are now going to take food out of their mouths by stealing the "perfect" job out from under them. I have seen more students humblebragging and negging their classmates than I care to remember, all in an effort to beat everyone to the finish line, to psych everyone else out, and ultimately to make themselves feel like they are just as competitive as everyone else. It is toxic and repulsive and can make the last bit of time you spend with your friends really unpleasant. You have absolutely no idea what is going on inside somebody's head, and you also have no idea what their life is like. So, while you are bragging about the great interview you just had with Amazing Brooklyn Design Studio, the person you are sitting next to might have sent out one hundred résumés and not heard back from anyone, and they are starting to panic and get depressed. You should be proud of yourself, you should be happy you got that great interview, but what you should not do is shove that information into somebody's face by bragging about it. All that accomplishes is stroking your ego, while possibly making your classmates—you're friends, remember?—feel horrible and worthless.

That is why it is so incredibly important to remember: nobody "wins" design school. Design school is not a contest. There is no first place (and the only thing being awarded valedictorian proves is that the person was good at getting AS in their classes). You are all in it together. Once you leave school, you are all out there in the profession together. Yes, you may be applying for the same jobs as your buddy, and yes, there are a limited number of openings at Amazing Brooklyn Design Studio, but there are always other jobs. There are always opportunities to work somewhere else. However, once you destroy a friendship by backstabbing a classmate to get the "best" job, there is rarely any way back from that. And what happens if ten years from now, that former classmate who hates you ends up working at the place you want to work? Do you think that they will speak highly of you? Do you think if they hear about an opening, they will reach out to the person who burned them senior year? Design is a tiny, tiny community, and you being a jerk senior year will, one way or another, come back to bite you in your ass.

The truth is that everyone is just as scared and nervous as you. Everyone is worried about the future, including those who already have jobs. Most of them don't want to move back in with their parents. They are worried about how they will pay their loans back, too. The transition from school to work is frightening. It is stressful. Once you remember this, then it gets easier to do what all seniors in a class should do: support one another. If you hear about a job you don't want, tell your classmates about it! If you know a company is hiring for something you are not qualified for, pass it on! Your classmates are the people you worked with, sweated with, learned software with, kerned type with, made models with, designed apps with, and generally created and learned with for the last four (or more) years—so please treat each other with kindness. Be proud of your accomplishments, but try to keep your business to yourself. Some of your classmates have not gotten any interviews yet and don't need to know that Apple is moving you to Silicon Valley and giving you a Tesla and unlimited avocados. Bragging is not needed. Kindness is.

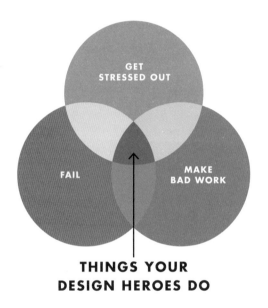

GET
STRESSED OUT

FAIL

MAKE
BAD WORK

**THINGS YOUR
DESIGN HEROES DO**

CHAPTER NINETEEN

HEROES

As a student at design school, you were exposed to a lot of design work. You likely took at least one, and maybe two or three classes in the history of art and design. You were shown and lectured on a lot of historical precedent as it relates to contemporary work. As somebody who is curious about design, you see work on the Internet all the time, and you have some favorite artists and designers you admire and appreciate. In fact, you probably have some heroes of design: people who you think are nothing short of brilliant in the work they make and their creative practice. These are people you look at with a sense of awe and wonder at how amazing their work is and how incredible their portfolios are.

Heroes are good. Looking up to another designer, admiring them, and wanting to eventually get to their level is a good thing to do. It can help to see how others did it before you, the road they took to get where they are. It can help you understand what it takes to be successful in this field. Heroes can provide a sense of hope that can be good to have, especially on the days you're not having fun being a designer.

What is not a good thing to do is to think of them as gods. You should not worship them. It is not good to think that everything they do is amazing and without fault, that they are flawless and consistently brilliant in their work. This is bad because quite simply it isn't true. Every single designer you like has made horrible, awful, crappy work. And I don't just mean when they started out, I mean right now. Everybody makes crap, and nobody is immune from making awful stuff, no matter how successful or well-known they are. Your heroes have crappy days where nothing is clicking. Your heroes make stuff that turns out horribly, and they have wasted a whole bunch of time getting nowhere. Your heroes have ideas that when fleshed out just don't work. This happens every single day to all the people you admire. Just because they are your heroes does not mean they never suck at being a designer, because they do.

Nobody is beyond criticism; nobody is so good that other people don't get to dislike what they make. Nobody is so perfect and so incredible at what they do that every single thing they make is unbelievably amazing. There is literally no one like that on the planet. Thinking about these people as untouchable is both ridiculous and toxic. It creates a completely unattainable fantasy world of what you think being a "good" designer is. It makes being that good into something you can never achieve— because they haven't gotten there either. It does not exist. You have an illusion of their amazingness in your head and it is simply not real. I see hero worship over and over and over again with students and professionals alike. People comparing themselves to their heroes and thinking, "I'll never be that good. I'll never make work that amazing." What everyone forgets is that their heroes once were in exactly the same spot they are now, and they once said the exact same thing about the work of their own heroes.

What you're not seeing is, as they say, the sausage getting made. You're not seeing all the mistakes, all the screw-ups, all the things that don't work, all the ideas that were horrible and misguided from the start. You are also not seeing all the time they have spent on these projects, the hours and hours and hours of refinement and changes and tweaking and alterations and time spent getting these pieces to where they look amazing. Even though you intellectually understand that this work does take time, you didn't have to live it, so you don't really reckon with it when you just see the end result. The other thing that you don't see is the years spent getting to the point of making good work. Your older heroes especially may have spent decades getting to where they are able to create that one beautiful piece you liked on Instagram.

The other thing you're not seeing on social media is their lives. I do not mean their lives that are carefully curated for getting likes, where they sip expensive coffee in a café in Venice or look pensively out at a sunrise over the mountains of Switzerland. I mean their actual, real lives. When they have to pay taxes, when they cook a normal, non-photogenic dinner, when their car breaks down, when they try to fall asleep, when they have an argument with their spouse, when they have bad breath—all the mediocre, uninteresting crap that goes along with being alive. In other words, you are not seeing all of the stuff that they don't post on social media, because it is just not that interesting. What you are seeing—and what you are comparing your own success to—is the highly curated, highly processed, most interesting, most awesome, most cool, and most visually appealing 2 percent of their lives.

When you start moving forward in your career, something interesting might happen: people might start looking at you as a hero. If this happens—and I hope it does, because it is an amazing feeling—you should be honest about the good stuff and the bad stuff. Instead of tucking the bad stuff away, you should feel free to talk about it. I have a large following on social media, and I often talk openly about my mental health, my struggles, when I'm having good days, when I'm having bad days, and just the reality of living beyond the carefully curated pictures of my work. I take the responsibility of having people listen to me very seriously. I think I owe it to them and to myself to be open and upfront about who I am. This lets people understand I am not a god, I am not infallible, I do not always make awesome stuff, I am a screwed-up, messed-up person trying to figure it out every day, feeling like I'm not ready, feeling just like they do. I hope you do the same.

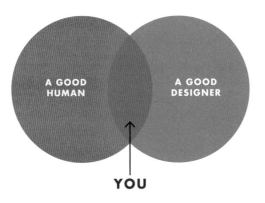

CHAPTER TWENTY

WHO ARE YOU?

I am going to end this book with an idea that I want you to keep in mind as both a student and a professional — something incredibly important that is unfortunately rarely talked about in school. As a designer, you shape and define the world around you. You make ideas into actual visual and physical things, and you help to create the context and environment that society exists in. All of which is to say this: designers make culture visual. Therefore, you have an enormous and serious ethical responsibility baked into your work, and you need to be very aware of it and keep it in mind as you make decisions. You have no doubt heard the saying "With great power comes great responsibility" — that is very true for designers.

We have all been taught that we should try to be caring, thoughtful, and kind people in our lives, and we should try to be caring, thoughtful, and kind people in our design work as well. The clients you choose to work with, the companies you join, the projects that you choose, the vendors and other people you collaborate with or outsource work to—all of these things count and all of these things affect our culture; therefore, all of these things demand a level of ethical integrity. In an effort to be inclusive, I'm not going to get political and take specific sides in this book (you can find me on social media for that)—but if you decide to work for companies, clients, or organizations that spread hate and fear, hurt people, and make the world a worse place— *you* are responsible for that. You are culpable and that is on your shoulders as much as it is on the people paying you. "But I just did what the client wanted" is not an acceptable excuse. You are responsible for the work you put out, and it is up to you as the designer to help your client understand the messaging and meaning of your output, for better or worse.

As I have said before in this book: design is not neutral. Your work says something, even if you think your work just says that you like getting a paycheck. Art and design not only shape the world, but also offer a critique of it. This is not something you should try to avoid—in fact, it is exactly the opposite: we have an enormous opportunity, and responsibility, to change things. Does this mean that using one typeface over another typeface makes the world a better place? No, it does not. Designers have a tendency to overinflate their egos, and I'm not trying to suggest that using one color over another slightly different color in a project will make the world a better place. What I am suggesting is that over time, your choices as a designer—and, more important, our collective choices as a community of designers—do affect our world. We bear a responsibility because as an industry, we really do change how things are. This can be something as simple as designing websites that work for people who are colorblind, using photography that is inclusive of different kinds of people, not taking a job with a xenophobic organization—or as complex as starting a nonprofit to help underrepresented communities or creating projects that help people overcome trauma in their lives.

I understand that you have to pay the bills. I understand that there is a very good chance you will have a lot of student loans to pay off. I understand that you want to buy stuff, live in a nice place, be able to eat dinner out with your friends, travel, and have a cool car. All of these things are completely valid. However, they do not negate the fact that you need to make some ethical choices in who you work for. Sometimes, you may need to do work you don't like, or work for a studio you're not excited about, or even do work that represents things you have a general dislike of—that is reasonable. But there must be a breaking point when it comes to doing work for people and for companies that hurt the world. You have to make a choice, there has to be a point where you say,

"No, I will not do that." Everybody has to decide for themselves where that point is—it is not up to me. You are the one who has to look at yourself in the mirror in the morning; how are you going feel about what you see? For every job you take, every project you make, every client you work with, you always want to know what it will pay, but you also need to ask what it will cost.

All of this is why it is so incredibly important not to bury your head in the sand and only care about design. You need to be a citizen of the world, not just a citizen of design. I'm not saying you need to be obsessive about the news, but you should know what's going on. It is important to understand the context for your work, to be aware of what people are doing and feeling, and to see what is happening out there, not just what is happening in your studio. The world is bigger than your font collection. There are so many more important things than picking exactly the right color for your website header. In order to make the world better, you have to understand what makes the world worse.

As a designer, you really can make the world different than how it is right now. So, go out there, and make it better.

BE A GOOD
HUMAN.
CONSIDER
EVERYTHING.
DEVELOP STRONG,
INFORMED OPINIONS.
DECIDE WHAT IS
MOST IMPORTANT
TO YOU.
MAKE THINGS
LIKE THEY MATTER.

ACKNOWLEDGMENTS

First and foremost I want to thank my family—for
always supporting me, for always being there when
I needed help, for always pushing me when I became lazy,
and for always believing in me. This book (and my entire
career) would never have happened without them.

Thank you to the team at Princeton Architectural
Press, including publisher Lynn Grady, design director
Paul Wagner, production director Janet Behning, prepress
manager Valerie Kamen, executive editor Jennifer
Thompson, and senior editor Sara Stemen for their
assistance in making this book a reality.

Next I want to thank all of you—all the people
I have gotten to speak with about design, teaching, art,
movies, food, music, and life in general. Everyone I have
met at other schools, at workshops, at conferences, at
lectures, and online, and all of my friends in Rochester
and across the globe. Our many conversations have
helped to solidify the ideas in this book.

Thank you to the faculty, staff, and administration at Rochester Institute of Technology, not for only allowing me the time and space to write a book, but also for the endless curiosity and excitement to see it made real—their endless supply of positive energy was infectious!

Finally I want to thank all of my teachers and all of my students. The amount that I have learned from you cannot be overstated—this book is not only for you, it is also *from* you. Thank you for your attention, your work, and your curiosity. My hope this that this book can help pay it forward in some small way.

ABOUT THE AUTHOR

Mitch Goldstein is a designer, artist, educator, and author based in upstate New York. He is an associate professor at Rochester Institute of Technology, where he teaches in the College of Art and Design. Over the past eighteen years, he has taught at Rhode Island School of Design, Virginia Commonwealth University, Maryland Institute College of Art, and other institutions. Mitch also maintains a creative practice focusing on various disciplines such as graphic design, wet darkroom photography, sculpture, and furniture design. He also writes and speaks about art and design education, pedagogy, and creative practice. He received his MFA in design and visual communications from Virginia Commonwealth University's School of the Arts, and his BFA in graphic design from Rhode Island School of Design.

www.mitchgoldstein.com

Published by
Princeton Architectural Press
A division of Chronicle Books LLC
70 West 36th Street
New York, New York 10018
papress.com

Printed and bound in China
26 25 24 23   4 3 2 1 First edition

ISBN 978-1-7972-2229-5

Editor: Jennifer N. Thompson
Designer: Mitch Goldstein

Library of Congress Control Number: 2022942792